A DUTIFUL BOY

A memoir of a gay Muslim's journey to acceptance

Mohsin Zaidi

◪ SQUARE PEG

3 5 7 9 10 8 6 4

Square Peg, an imprint of Vintage,
20 Vauxhall Bridge Road,
London SW1V 2SA

Square Peg is part of the Penguin Random House group of companies
whose addresses can be found at global.penguinrandomhouse.com

 Penguin
Random House
UK

First published by Square Peg in 2020

Penguin.co.uk/vintage

A CIP catalogue record for this book is available from the British Library

Hardback ISBN 9781529110142
Trade paperback ISBN 9781529110159

Typeset in 10/18 pt Miller Text
by Integra Software Services Pvt. Ltd, Pondicherry

Printed and bound in Great Britain by Clays Ltd, Elcograf S.p.A.

Penguin Random House is committed to a sustainable future for
our business, our readers and our planet. This book is made from
Forest Stewardship Council® certified paper.

MIX
Paper from
responsible sources
FSC   FSC® C018179
www.fsc.org

For Mamu Tier, the uncle every child should have.
For my niece, Aya bear, in the hope she never
needs me the way I need him.

And to every young person struggling with their identity.
You are not alone.

Author's Note

The names and other identifying features of some people, places and events have been changed or merged in order to ensure that they are not identifiable so as to protect the privacy of individuals. This is a story based on memories of my experiences.

Not everything that is faced can be changed,
but nothing can be changed until it is faced.

James Baldwin, 14 January 1962

Prologue

Her promise to meet him was only to placate me. It was hollow like our love had become. For ten years my mum had resisted. Fought against the idea as though she were holding off an army at the castle gates, and yet, here we were. A day I thought would never come. The drawbridge about to lower.

In battle, are you ever really ready for the white flag? In the moment, the focus is on the fight, so when surrender comes, the impact of it might leave you dumbfounded. But my plan had worked. I'd played the long game and won. My heart didn't jump for joy or skip a beat. It lay inert and heavy in my chest.

My boyfriend and I would visit her and my dad at their home. A home from which it felt like so much of me had been exiled. Now, though, we would both go there to eat Pakistani food, cooked with her hands, with her history. Tastes from a faraway place to usher in an equally foreign concept.

My parents lived in a London suburb six stops east from Mile End on the Central Line. Those six stops were almost as familiar to me as the family home itself. Usually, I travelled alone and, at each stop, a part of me would fall away. At Stratford, I would forget what they had said to me. At Leyton, I would discard what they had done. By Leytonstone, I'd put down the anger I felt towards Islam, dear to them and once so dear to me. At Snaresbrook, I'd suppress my anger towards them. Then South Woodford, the penultimate stop. That's where I would leave behind what I cherished most of all: my love for him. To take it with me would have been to disrespect, to demean it.

On this day, though, no part of me would be left behind. Not my love for him and not him either. Not his whiteness or the sharp blue of his eyes. If only I could dim the bright blue, which I loved so much, just for that evening. Make him smaller, moulded to fit neatly into their closed hearts.

Hours before we left, I lay on the bed feeling as blank as the ceiling I stared at. I couldn't do it, I told him. As I spoke cracks formed in my numb veneer, beneath it a seething rage. I told him I was sorry. And I was sorry. I was desperate to go through with it, but consumed by anger towards her, at myself and at the rules that had built a wall between us.

But then we were on our way, on a train heading for the unknowable. I held on to him more tightly as we got closer, for once hanging on to those things I had become so accustomed to leaving behind. We stood outside the house. Two men. My dad opened the door. I asked him where she was, and his frown made my heart sink.

PART ONE

1

My dad's back was shredded and covered in blood. He had done this to himself. In front of me. I was seven. On the first nine evenings of the ten holiest days in the Shia Muslim calendar, my family and I would join the rest of our community at mosque, separated by gender, to beat at our chests with our hands. Standing in a wide circle under fluorescent tubes emitting a cheap, bright light, the most impassioned beaters would huddle at the front, topless, in the hope of inflicting just a little more pain. Bodies leaning back, hands raised high in the air, held there for a moment to gather momentum, then whipped down onto reddening brown torsos. Perfectly in sync with one another and with the Urdu words that rushed out of my jolted lungs. The methodical sound of skin slapping skin, escalating in my head and urging me to beat harder. But on the tenth day, in the car park of the mosque located just off a busy east London road, the grown-ups would use blades rather than hands.

My dad, who would do anything for his faith, gripped a black handle that fastened together three small chains connected to long silver blades. They glistened in the light, like a child's plaything. I gripped my little brother's hand, the two of us standing with other spectators. Members of St John's Ambulance stood by, watching in disbelief, unable to rationalise what they were seeing. I was more enthralled by their reactions than those blades. Those I had seen before; the disapproving shock on these white faces I had not. They seemed scared but they had nothing to be scared of. My dad, fiercely devout, might do this to himself but he would never hurt anyone else. They blinked each time the knife struck skin, as if the pouring blood had splattered into their eyes. I stared at my dad's back as he screamed. It was an emotional shriek, not a pained one, followed by another and another and another. Blood flying through the air, landing on people's clothes and my face, staining my memories red. His eyes were shut as he continued to rip apart his back. Crimson streams traced lines down his torso, towards his legs. He looked in my direction. I do this for you, my son, and one day you will do this for me, he said without a word. Among the clattering of blades, I felt a sense of excitement, a sense of belonging to a small group of only the most devout Shias, those closest to God. A belonging that would grow stronger as I grew older. Strong enough that, one day, I too could shed blood and live.

To me, Shia Islam was not just a religion. It was not simply a set of rules. And it was not a belief. Like other religions it was an all-encompassing world, into which I was born. With its own history, its own calendar, its own food, clothes, traditions, books, maths, laws and even its own deviants. The first words whispered into my ear on the day of my birth were the same as those heard by every Muslim baby, they were of the Kalma, telling me there was one God and that the Prophet Muhammad was his messenger. Islam's borders transcended geographical boundaries. On one side were people like me, who carried the faith in their hearts. On the other side were infidels (non-believers). There was no such thing as a dual identity. My only anthem was the call to prayer that rang out into each corner and every eardrum five times a day. The *azaan*, the same poetic ancient Arabic tones that had flown purposefully across mountains and oceans for over fourteen hundred years, seeking out followers of the prophet.

Before I could walk, my parents taught me to lower myself into prayer, mimicking their greetings as they met with their God. Unlike the majority of Muslims, who hold their hands together, my parents prayed with their hands by their sides. We were a minority, told by other Muslims that our violence, albeit self-inflicted, meant we were not Muslim at all. We were under attack and so my parents instilled the importance of holding on to my identity more firmly, fearing that, unless I did, it might be taken away.

As a Muslim it was expected that I read the Quran in its original ancient Arabic at least once before I die. Mastering the language and the holy book's 114 chapters took years. Every day after primary school, I spent two hours at Quran classes, held on a white bed sheet, spread across a local Shia woman's tiled kitchen floor. A brimless round white cap slipped off my head as I dragged my feet to class. Glimpses of my black hair burst through the patterned holes. I surreptitiously glanced at the girls in hijabs on the other side of the room, as we rocked back and forth while studying the Arabic patterns that went from right to left. Taught to read aloud words with no sense of their meaning, the sounds made little impression on my immature ears. A long, transparent, plastic ruler policed my thoughts, whacked firmly down in front of me by the teacher when my humming stopped, and my mind got up and hopped towards cartoons and dinner.

My grandmother from Pakistan spoke of Islam often during her visits to the UK. 'Mohsin, Allah is with you always. He will always be there to guide you,' she said as she ate rice with her hands. My parents told me stories of the two invisible little angels who lived on my shoulders. The angel that lived on the right kept a list of all the good things I did. The angel on the left, a list of the bad. I imagined them as two tiny white men.

Perhaps if I spoke Urdu they wouldn't understand? At night, while I slept, the angels would sneak up to heaven to report my daily deeds and misdeeds back to Allah. While I was on the toilet the angels would leave the room out of politeness. I could see them scurry out when my hand touched the zip of my trousers.

Such tales were common, but one in particular haunted me. My parents recalled seeing a woman frantically flagging them down for help on an unlit, deserted road at dawn. Concerned for her safety they pulled over and got out of the car, but she'd vanished – there was no one to be found in the early-morning light. They were sure it was a jinn, a rebellious little demon spirit born out of a smokeless fire in Islamic mythology. Although jinn possess supernatural qualities and I had never actually seen one, their four limbs, dangerous faces and animal-like traits were as real to me as the floor on which I walked, as the omnipotent God to whom I prayed.

I was told that jinn coexisted with humans but on a spiritual plane. Jinn had the power to inhabit human bodies. When somebody was mentally unwell, demon possession was the cause and exorcism the cure. At night I passed the tree near our front door slowly, taking care not to let its swaying branches out of my sight. Do not, however desperate you may be, urinate on trees, my dad warned. Trees were the home of the jinn and were to be treated with the utmost respect. In the moonlight, the shadows of jinn pacing between branches seemed to illuminate the walls of my bedroom, and a parasitic fear of possession burrowed into me.

My parents taught me that Muharram, the Islamic month that marked the anniversary of the martyrdom of the Prophet Muhammad's family, was a month of grieving for the slaughter of our people. We experienced pain to feel closer to theirs. I dressed entirely in black. I didn't play music because it was a time for mourning. Each night of the first ten days, I attended the local Shia mosque, a Victorian former post office building with a red-brick exterior that sat in the heart of Walthamstow. The entrance was scattered with the shoes of men, women and children: the only place where the sexes would mingle, along with the smell of feet. Inside, inadequate electric heaters churned out warmth that quickly dissipated up to a ceiling decorated with rusting, interconnecting iron bars and slanted panel windows that let in the icy air. A series of white bed sheets covered the cold concrete floor. To the side of the entrance was a special bathroom for the purification ritual performed before each prayer. I had been taught to use water to clean out the sins lodged beneath my fingernails and within my thoughts.

A children's sermon took place before the main one. At it they told simplified tales of angels and prophets. One story involved a 'non-believer'. It was told by a teenage boy who considered himself a pious man in waiting.

'What if the non-believer is a really good person?' I asked, without waiting to be called on. I was thinking of Superman. Superman was my hero. He wasn't Muslim but he helped everybody. The young preacher smiled sympathetically in my direction.

'They still won't go to heaven,' he replied, shaking his head gently, as if damning somebody to eternal hellfire was as straightforward as saying yes or no to a cup of tea.

'OK ...' the cogs in my seven-year-old mind still turning, 'but what if you have a non-believer who is better than a Muslim? Then what happens?' His arms now crossed as he sat up to look at me more purposefully.

'The Muslim will answer to Allah for his behaviour. The non-believer will be punished for failing to embrace Islam,' he said, in a tone slightly sharper than before.

That still didn't sound fair. 'OK ... What if you get a non-believer who has been really, *really* good and never heard of Islam. What happens to them?'

Frustrated with my childish inquisitiveness, he snapped back: 'That wouldn't happen these days because of technology,' and then he moved on.

As we were ushered into the men's hall for the main sermon, the conversation left me uncomfortable, like I had swallowed something without chewing.

A mullah, trained in oratory as well as Islam, captivated his male audience, while my mum and other women watched on a small TV next door. He told stories in a sophisticated Urdu intended for immigrants but not their native-born children. My Urdu was better than my English until I went to school. When I was still at nursery, I spoke to all white people with the few English words I knew and to everyone else in Urdu. But soon, English prevailed and my home language became muddled.

From what I could glean, the mullah told tales of horrendous violence met with tremendous courage. And on the tenth day, the tale reached its climax. That evening, the lights in the mosque were turned off. I could see the place crammed with the silhouettes of men, sat uncomfortably side by side, row after row. As the orator's voice filled the room with his words of bloodshed and devastation, tears escalated into whimpers that became wails. Each year I had heard the same story. I closed my eyes and clenched my fists, trying with all of my life force to summon just one tear. Nothing. I could only picture Superman. He wouldn't go to hell, I was sure. How could being good not be good enough? Suddenly the lights came on and we took to our feet so that, once again, the self-flagellation could begin.

2

It was the 1992 cricket world cup final and it was *them* against *us*. White versus brown. Christian versus Muslim. Rich versus poor. England versus Pakistan. I watched, aged seven, from the small living room of my aunt's terraced house in Walthamstow. I chanted, praying for Pakistan, an unfamiliar place. My parents, brother, cousins, aunties and uncles collectively cheered for the handsome Imran Khan. The green of the captain's shirt mirrored that of the flag I had wrapped around me, with a large white crescent and five-rayed star at its centre, designed under the watchful eye of the British Raj, my dad told me, to symbolise Islam and the rights of religious minorities and light and progress.

My dad told us that Imran had gone to a place called 'Oxford'. I didn't know what that was but apparently we had driven there and seen it from the outside once. I couldn't be sure because from the way the word delicately left my dad's mouth each time he said it, it seemed other-worldly.

After Pakistan's victory, hundreds of crescents and stars in a sea of green danced on Walthamstow's streets to the sound of car horns and loud Bollywood music blasting from halal meat shops. We were joyous in the defeat of the land on which our homes stood, but not our hearts. Although where did mine belong if not Walthamstow? There were only a few English people in the crowds. One man looked both confused and disgusted and an inexplicable guilt overcame me. 'You're in England!' I heard him shout, before he shuffled away shaking his head. England. The country I lived in but knew little of.

'Your grandad was invited here because those English people needed workers in their factories and then, as soon as we arrived, they wanted us to leave!' my nan said. She told me they left Pakistan seeking a better life for their children.

Neither of my parents was born in England. They met only six times before their arranged – not forced – marriage and together planted the seed of themselves in the country's soil, in the hope that it would grow.

'It's six more times than any of your grandparents got,' my dad explained to me through a smirk brought on by the foreignness of his son's disbelief. Theirs was the first Asian wedding in Northampton, the town my mum had moved to from Pakistan at the age of six. The story of my nan cooking food for two hundred people, a modest wedding by Pakistani standards, had been committed to the family archive as one of its proudest moments and was recalled at every wedding thereafter.

A picture of my mum and dad, newlywed, standing side by side was the centrepiece in a local paper and now the centrepiece in our living room. My dad, with his dark brown skin, straight black hair and moustache, wears a navy suit, with a red tie and red carnation in his lapel. In the photo my mum is beaming, her fair complexion highlighted by red lipstick and waves of dark brown hair held back with a matching red carnation. Her red-and-gold sari is intricately stitched from top to bottom, complementing her fine features. She had the height and glamour of an Indian film star, but her big brown eyes had seen a life that was anything but Bollywood. Eyes that I inherited, and a life that she didn't want me to. She was confined by circumstance, leaving school at sixteen to provide for her parents and younger siblings. The people she went to school with labelled her 'Fatpak' on account of her being both Pakistani and plump as a teen. Racist taunts in a 70s England still unused to immigrants, forcing her to seek refuge with the few other ethnics at her school, namely three black girls. The four of them commandeered their otherness and used it as a protective cloak, taking advantage of it to appear aggressive, because, she told me, what else could a group of non-whites be?

Like most of the other Pakistanis we knew, my parents didn't have much. Immediately after their marriage they were on a list of people in need of council housing. By tradition they would have moved in with my dad's parents but they were in Pakistan. While my parents waited for something more permanent, they moved into a small room above the fried-chicken shop where my dad worked. It had four walls and a sink but no heating. A woman who visited from the local authority took pity on my mum – I was a babe in her arms –and she listened as Mum pleaded with her not to place us in one of the brutal tower blocks that dotted the Walthamstow skyline.

The Victorian terraced house I grew up in, provided to us by the local council, felt huge until I visited Dad's friend whose home was double-fronted. Being able to walk into a house and go left or right blew my mind. My mum and dad's bedroom looked onto the street. I shared a bedroom with my younger brother and his countless posters of Arsenal FC players. He was born ten and a half months after me but in the same year. Our single beds within poking distance of each other. The kitchen was the centre of our house, from which the aroma of Eastern spices and the sound of Western voices filled our home. The garden was a patch of concrete where my brother and I played.

'Tier ... I mean ... Zain ... I mean ... Mohsin, Abbass,' my mum shouted, calling us in for dinner, often mistakenly first using the names of her younger brothers, my uncles, to whom she had been a second mother. We ate together each day at the kitchen table, where the character of a person was measured by the amount of spice they could handle. The same table at which heated discussions took place about things like whether a Bollywood film without songs could be a Bollywood film.

'No songs?!' was the phrase repeated by each of us, emphasising the disapproval, reacting as if breaking into song was integral to life. Our lives did not pause for music. Perhaps that's why it was so important that the ones we watched on screen did.

Next door on one side lived a white family. The parents didn't go to work. The mother smoked while she was pregnant which my mum told me was very naughty. Their two boys and a girl were slightly younger than us. Fair and blue-eyed, they looked angelic but for their stained and unwashed clothes. Next door on the other side was a house where every room was rented separately. There were frequent comings and goings, some for sex and others for drugs. A thin brick wall separated our houses, and the frequent crashes and thuds and screams and groans kept me awake at night.

My dad had a business degree from Pakistan and now worked in a branch of an international bank, BCCI, until he discovered from the six o'clock news that the bank had collapsed. He frowned at the TV and then looked to my mum. Her eyes were fixed on the screen and one hand clasped her forehead as the newsreader informed them that the life they had only recently taken out of the packaging would not be kind.

The job loss forced us to move to Northampton for the summer holidays but my dad stayed in London, job hunting. While my mum packaged chocolate in the Cadbury's factory nearby, my nan looked after me and Abbass. Each evening, as I heard the front door of my nan's terraced house open, I ran to it, excited to see my mum but more excited by yet another bar of Cadbury's that I would wrestle Abbass for. These bars had been rejected from the factory line and given to staff, so we ended up with Twirls with no twirls or Flakes that did not flake.

I loved living with my nan. She was a seamstress and worked on her machine at home. Knowing how much I loved Superman, she surprised me with a cape with the golden 'S' on the back and I wore it everywhere. The cape made me feel strong.

The only English my nan spoke was to ask for a 'fish bugger' from McDonald's, which made my mum's brothers, Tier and Zain, laugh for some reason. They took care of us the way our mum had taken care of them when they were kids. Although Nan was home, she was busy with Grandad who had been depressed for as long as I could remember. He seldom spoke and spent a lot of time washing his hands in the bathroom. Once I almost weed myself waiting for him to finish.

My uncles were in their late teens and went out on the town every Friday and Saturday night. In the early evenings, nineties dance music blasted from the front room. Uncle Tier secretly ushered me in, an audience to his dancing. I gazed up at him as he swayed and bit his bottom lip, telling me that club promoters asked him to dance on podiums because he could do this and this and this. I wanted to get up and dance too but it seemed like the wrong thing to do. The difference between the way my parents told me to behave and the moves on display in front of me was confusing and made it feel like there was much of my world that made no sense.

3

We moved back to our terraced house in Walthamstow after the summer when my mum's job in the factory came to an end and we had to go back to school. My London was the local street market – the longest in Europe – with stalls selling batteries, cheap toys, cheap clothes. There was also Green Street for Eid, Southall for the best Pakistani food and Oxford Street on special occasions. In our predominantly Pakistani area, overrun with fried-chicken takeaways, halal butchers and Asian clothes shops, we used the Urdu word for Aryan, *goreh*, to describe white people, who inhabited a parallel, more desirable city and a more desirable skin. I thought of them as something to aspire to. I was an English-born child but I sensed that I did not live in the England I saw on TV.

The local sweet shop was at the end of our road. After summer, Abbass and I had been allowed to go together, with my mum watching from the front door. I couldn't wait to be a grown-up and these felt like my first independent steps. But then Stephen Lawrence was murdered by racists. It was all over the news, all of the time and, suddenly, getting a little older meant feeling a little less safe. My parents vetoed any further trips to the shop alone, saying that these were dangerous times.

We had no money but my dad refused to accept government benefits. 'I will not take handouts from this country,' he said. I could sense his frustration. That's what *they* wanted him to do, so that *they* could judge him for it, he told me. Aged eight, I couldn't understand why the government would give us money for free, let alone why my dad would refuse it. Money was this thing that we always needed but never seemed to have. Late one night, the soft light coming through my bedroom door frame told me my mum was still up. I crept out as quietly as I could so as not to disturb Abbass and found her kneeling on the kitchen floor, loading clothes into the washing machine. I was used to seeing her do this during the day because afterwards I would hand her the wet clothes to peg onto the line in the garden, still too high up for me to reach myself.

'Ami, why are you doing laundry in the middle of the night?' I asked. She smiled and explained.

'Because of something called "economy 7", Mochie –' that was her nickname for me – 'it means that electricity is cheaper at night-time which helps us save money.'

I went back upstairs and fell asleep to excited thoughts of how many new toy wrestlers I would get now that we had economy 7.

My dad said companies mistrusted a foreigner's CV. Until he got what he called a proper job, he drove a minicab. He worked, he got paid. What was improper about that? My mum started a nursery course at the local college, hoping that, once she qualified, she would find a job nearby. Maybe one day we'd go back to Pakistan as a family and they would open their own nursery.

The prospect of driving around London all day instead of going to school filled me with excitement. Sometimes, I would feign illness as my mum got ready for college, leaving her with no choice but to call my dad, who, having left for work at dawn, would have to come and get me.

We collected customers from one place and took them to another. I wasn't allowed to speak unless spoken to otherwise no McDonald's for lunch. I could only eat Filet-O-Fish because the Big Mac wasn't halal. That didn't stop me dribbling at the thought of one though. The white people didn't usually talk to me or to Dad but I loved it when they did. We once collected a man who looked much the same as other white men, but his eyes seemed kinder to me. He asked my dad to take him to a mosque.

'Why are you going to a mosque?' I asked. I'd never seen a white person in a mosque.

'Mohsin! I ... I'm sorry, please ignore him,' my dad interjected. I turned away, sinking into my seat.

'That's OK,' the man said. I turned round again quickly, grabbing the back of my seat, all ears. 'I'm going to read namaz.'

'You can't be Muslim, you're not Pakistani,' I said.

'Mohsin!' I was definitely not getting a Filet-O-Fish later.

After we dropped the man off, my dad explained that Muslims were not just from Pakistan. That there were also English Muslims and black Muslims (to us English meant white). This news was as bewildering to me as the sky turning neon green. For the rest of the day I remained silent, wondering which of the passengers was also a Muslim like me. When I told Abbass that evening, he couldn't believe it either.

During these trips, my dad pointed out Big Ben and Trafalgar Square and I felt like I was on holiday, seeing the places which, until then, only existed on a Monopoly board. I could tell it was not so pleasant for him though. He grew increasingly distant from the family, as if he were ashamed of something I could not see. He was a proud man and driving people from A to B made him miserable. He sometimes mentioned to passengers he'd collected from outside banks that he used to work at one himself. They seldom said very much in reply.

When he wasn't driving, my dad was job hunting but nothing seemed to work out. After a series of phone calls with his best friend from university, my dad decided to return to Pakistan. My uncle Makki had set up a chain of successful restaurants in Lahore. He and my dad weren't related but in Pakistani culture he was still my uncle.

When I asked Mum why Dad was leaving, she said it was because he was trying to take care of us but that made no sense to me.

'I'm going back home, Mochie,' my dad said.

'But this is our home, Dad,' I replied.

'No, *betah*, this is not our home. We are guests here. Our home is with our people, in a Muslim country where the *azaan* can be heard five times a day wherever you are.' I secretly liked that the call to prayer didn't play before sunrise every morning in Walthamstow. He planned to move in with Uncle Makki and build a new life out there. We would follow him or he would send money back but he couldn't stay in a London of closed doors any longer.

By contrast, doors seemed to be opening for my mum. She qualified with a distinction from her nursery course and the course teacher insisted she go on to university. Her exceptional talent would be wasted otherwise, he said. My mum enrolled to study History at the University of East London. History because her brother Tier told her she'd love it after recently graduating with the same degree, the University of East London because it was the closest to home.

On the afternoon my dad was leaving to start a new life in Pakistan, Abbass packed all his belongings into thirteen carrier bags, including his teddies, and pleaded to go with him. I couldn't appreciate what my dad's absence would feel like; it was difficult to be upset about something that hadn't happened. I watched Abbass sob silently, his chubby face crinkled and red as my dad got into the car and was driven away. That night we slept with Mum in my parents' bed, my head tucked under one arm and Abbass, puffy-eyed from crying, nestled under the other.

My mum was not good at hiding her emotions and I could sense her vulnerability. That she didn't feel safe made me fear we were not. We survived off her student loan. Abbass was having nightmares and started to sleepwalk. He'd get out of bed, go to the edge of the room and cry, without once waking up. We began to sleep in my mum's bed every night, huddled together behind a locked bedroom door.

Uncle Tier and Uncle Zain took turns coming down from Northampton to London, so that we weren't alone. Having them there made our home feel secure again. My mum was less anxious. She was more like the mum when Dad was around.

The younger of her brothers, Uncle Zain, found my mannerisms amusing, in particular the way I spoke. After arriving in the UK, my mum spent a year in a nice town on the outskirts of London before her family moved to Northampton. My middle-class English accent, inherited from her, hid my East London origins. One morning, after some of my classmates heard her speaking to me, a couple of them told me she sounded even more white than I did. My voice belonged not to me but to a boy from the Home Counties. At my first parents' evening, the teacher told my mum that it was like having a little public-school boy in the class. Mum didn't quite know what that meant but nodded politely.

Uncle Zain was visiting and overheard me ask my mum whether we could put on Mariah Carey's 'Dreamlover' while we cleaned the house. We often blasted music as loud as our sound system could manage and tidied up as we sang along. He laughed and plucked from his mind a new nickname for me: Fag Bag. He used it from then on as a term of endearment when speaking to me or about me. It never crossed my mind to ask what it meant. 'Don't call him that, Zain,' my mum would say to him, only half seriously.

One day I wandered in from the garden to find Uncle Zain watching TV. A man with a moustache wearing a bright yellow jacket, white vest and white trousers was singing on the screen. The camera angle skipped behind him, to his silhouette, one arm stretched to the sky and the other clasped firmly to a microphone stand that was bending to his will, his voice projecting, so strong and deep, it seemed like the microphone was just a toy. I was fixated by this sparkling human being. The beat made me want to move my hips.

'Bloody deserved it, the poofter,' my uncle observed. 'Zain, don't say that!' my mum called from the kitchen.

'It's the gay disease. What did he expect?' he shouted back, half smiling as he looked at me.

'Not in front of the children, Zain!'

I didn't like what he was saying but brushed the feeling aside and went back into the garden to play with Abbass.

Although it felt like he'd been away longer, my dad returned from Pakistan a year later. Things hadn't worked out the way he'd planned and he had been lonely without us, he explained. He'd shaved off his moustache and my mum cried. Abbass hid behind her and refused to go near him. I was speechless. It was like seeing a cat without fur. You knew, somewhere deep down, that it was possible but it didn't make it any less ghastly in the flesh. I don't think it was the reception he had hoped for.

Uncle Makki visited soon after with his wife and three children, the eldest of whom, Mariam, was a year younger than me. Our guests wore designer clothes and returned home each evening with yet more shopping bags with funny names that I could not read.

Mariam and I became close. Our fathers had joked long before she and I were born that their children might one day be wed and our friendship seemed to turn these youthful fantasies into the seed of an idea. One of the many games Mariam and I played together involved a catalogue they had brought home from one of their shopping trips. We leafed through and on each page selected the one thing we would buy if money were no object, skipping quickly past the underwear section as Allah would expect us to.

When they went back to Pakistan, I noticed the catalogue had been left behind. I was instantly curious about the underwear section. I paused for a moment. Life, we had been taught, was a test and Allah was always watching. So were his angels, I remembered. But I reasoned that everyone had to shop for underwear so it couldn't be completely anti-Islamic to look. I sat down and turned the pages, ignoring the voice telling me to stop. I was staring at half-naked men and women though they seemed to be almost a different species from me. I'd never seen so much bare white flesh. I admired the way white skin seemed to glow. I didn't see that glow in my own complexion. We had dark hair, dark eyes, dark skin. They were light. The hair on their heads was a mixture of blonde and pale brown, their eyes blue and green. Their bodies were toned and muscled in a way that was as unfamiliar as it was enticing. They were smiling at me, and from those smiles, I knew that something about this was deeply wrong.

4

'Can I talk to you please?' The mother of one of the kids in my primary-school class cornered my mum in the playground after school. When I'd arrived at school that morning I thought I might have made a mistake because over half the class hadn't come in.

'Yes of course,' my mum replied in Urdu.

'Today they were learning about ... you know ... those things ... so we didn't send Marya to school. Most of us parents didn't. I'm here to complain. Did you not get the letter?'

I looked up at my mum who had folded her arms and pursed her lips.

'I got the letter,' she said evenly.

'Oh ... so you want your child to learn such things? You aren't worried about what these English people are teaching him?'

'I would rather he learn about these things properly, and not from other children or rumours or magazines. The school is teaching them about their bodies and I don't see any problem with it,' my mum said. The woman grumbled and shuffled away.

'Mochie, we have to get you out of here.'

It was 1996, and Walthamstow, one of the poorest areas in the country, did not have selective schools. Selection meant sitting tests that determined whether you would join fellow high performers at a grammar school or be thrown, at the tender age of ten or eleven, into a pile marked 'other' by being sent to a local comprehensive. The neighbouring council district of Redbridge was heaving with new cars and semi-detached houses. It had some of the best secondary schools in London, including a top-performing grammar school for boys. Redbridge parents were notified of the 'eleven-plus' entrance exam. Outsiders like us were not and, by just a day, my mum missed the registration deadline for me to sit the exam. As she drove Abbass and me from our desperate surroundings to the quaint-ness of Redbridge's clean, safe streets, she gripped the steering wheel ever tighter, fixed on our destination. She planned to explain and to plead and, if it was required of her, to beg for an extension to the deadline. Grammar school would place me in the England of opportunity, a place she had heard of but never seen. The England my dad had hoped but failed to find when he stepped off the plane.

Begging didn't work and tears overcame her as the council employee explained in a matter-of-fact tone that the rules were the rules and there was nothing he could do. He stared at her, willing her to move away from the desk.

Her tears confused and embarrassed me. I wanted to comfort her but she was too tall, her thoughts too far for me to reach. I looked on as she mourned the loss of her only opportunity to propel her elder son out of the deep ditch of poverty. But she would not be defeated.

'OK, let's move on,' he said. I wish I'd worn a tie, like the other boys. I'd never worn one before but now, without it, I felt almost naked. None of the words he used meant anything to me. I looked over at my mum, on the other side of the room, perched on the edge of an old wooden chair.

'He knows this!' my mum interjected.

'Please try and leave it to him, Mrs Zaidi,' he said. He was the head teacher of the private school I was interviewing for.

'Sorry.' My mum's desperation came from the fact that, to get into this private school, I would need a scholarship and to get a scholarship I had to be better than just *good enough*.

'What do you dream of being when you grow up, Mohsin?' the head asked. His eyes seemed to bore straight through me.

'I want to be a lawyer,' I replied confidently.

'A solicitor or a barrister?'

'Um ...' I didn't know the difference. 'I'm ... I'm not sure.'

'OK ... well ... Why do you want to be a lawyer?' He had become snappier as the interview progressed. He was running out of bones to throw me.

'I don't know,' I said. My mum and dad had told me I had to be a lawyer or a doctor and I wasn't very good at science or maths, but I couldn't tell him that.

He shrugged his shoulders lightly, lowered his chin to his chest and looked down at me, eyes peeking over the top of his reading glasses, poised on the tip of his nose. 'Put everything else to one side for me.' He glanced at my mum. 'What do you dream of becoming?'

Nobody had asked me this question before. He was urging me to show him a part of myself that he sensed might be there but couldn't yet be seen. I appeared to him as a blur and he wanted me to draw definite, pronounced lines around myself. The problem was I wouldn't know where to begin because I didn't dream of becoming anything. I wanted a job so that I could buy my mum presents and take care of my parents when they were old, but such dreams wouldn't be big enough for him and this school.

I failed the exams and the interview.

'So you'll be going to the school nearby, Mochie.' My mum looked defeated. The school did not have a good reputation but I was pleased because my walk would take less than five minutes. 'Are you OK?' she asked.

From her muted tone I could tell this was bad news and that I should be disappointed too. When I was sad, my mum would do an impression of Donald Duck that instantly brought a smile to my face. I wished I could do the same for her now.

'I'm OK,' I said, bowing my head to show disappointment, but the truth was, at eleven years old, I didn't care which school I went to.

'You.' My new form tutor was pointing at me as the unfamiliar faces of my new classmates stared.

'Stand up,' she said.

I rose slowly, holding on to my desk, my fingers finding a piece of old chewing gum beneath it.

'What is your name?' What had I done? I was only ten minutes into secondary school. My parents would kill me.

'Mohsin,' I replied.

'Mohsin,' she repeated. She was smiling. 'Your uniform is absolutely perfect. Well done.' I beamed; I couldn't wait to tell my mum and dad.

On the way to my first lesson, it began. 'Boffin!' a tall, broad-shouldered boy with short dreads shouted in my direction. Marlon was in my class and he stood with a group of other boys. They laughed.

'I don't know what that means,' I replied. He paused, obviously confused by the fact I'd replied at all.

'Teacher's pet,' he said, part insult, part explanation.

That night, and for many nights after, I lied to my parents when they asked how school was. I'd never lied to them before, and each time I did, I felt the weight of Allah's judgement on my tongue as the words left my mouth. I told them it was fine, that I was making friends and doing well in class. Only the last of those was true.

I was first mugged within a month of starting at my new school. I walked towards class and could smell smoke. The closer I got the stronger the smell. I stopped abruptly at the sound of whispering voices. Then a boy leapt out at me.

'What da fuck you doin, bruv? Oi, Riaz, look at this dickhead,' he said as he pulled me behind the classroom cabin. His bloodshot eyes were raging. They were older than me and also Pakistani. I was used to some of the black boys punching me but not them. In the little time I'd been at my new school I'd learned about the line between us and them. The Pakistanis had nicknames for the black boys: 'kaleh', which translated simply as blacks but was loaded with racism. Even in our school, which only had a handful of white kids, there was an unspoken racial hierarchy in the air.

'You better not tell anyone, yeah? We'll fuck you up!' Riaz said. They threw me to the floor and began kicking my ribcage. Riaz unzipped the front pocket of my rucksack, rummaging around, as if he could smell the money inside. They could see I was on the verge of tears. 'Don't worry ... you're lucky we didn't beat you more,' he said as they turned the corner, leaving me wedged between the bushes and my new classroom.

At school, if you wanted cigarettes or weed you went to Riaz. He had older brothers and apparently one of them was already in prison for drug dealing. No one messed with him because they'd have his brothers to deal with. That night I said nothing at the dinner table. Nothing about Riaz, nothing about school, nothing about the fact that I hadn't any lunch money for the rest of the week. By Friday I was distraught. The ball of anxiety I'd felt on my first day grew until it filled my stomach. My mum sat me down that evening and asked me if I was OK. As usual, I told her I was fine but this time she was unrelenting.

'Mochie, I know there is something going on. You have to tell me otherwise I can't help you.' She could help me. She could stop it. I didn't know how but I knew she could because my mum could do anything she put her mind to. She was now a teacher at a primary school and I thought she might understand the way things worked. I told her what had happened but asked her not to tell the school because Riaz would find out that I had snitched on him. Mum liked to be in control. The expression on her face was a mixture of helplessness and dread, as if I were in harm's way but she could do nothing about it. As I recounted what had happened, it was as if I was kicking her, shouting at her, forcing her to go through my attack. At the same time, I knew she would play it differently. My mum's family was from a place in Pakistan called Kulluwal. They were known for being tall and fair and fearless fighters with hot tempers. Mum was Kulluwal's daughter and I worried that my meekness disappointed her. That she might feel that not enough of her had made its way into me if I couldn't get angry and fight back. If all I could do was withdraw into myself for fear of upsetting everyone else.

A few weeks later, I saw Riaz by the school gates at the end of the day. He was waiting for me.

'You fucking little bastard – you know who I am? I'll fuck you up,' he was shouting, safe in the knowledge that no one would dare to intervene.

'I ... I ... don't know what you're talking about,' I said, but I did. Although I'd asked her not to I knew from the moment he started towards me that my mum had told the school. 'Yes you fucking do, you lying little cunt.' He punched me a few times until I fell. 'You say anything else to anyone and I swear I'll fuckin' stab you next time, yeah.' I believed him and did as I was told. If the abuse wasn't coming from him, it was from Marlon, and if it wasn't Marlon it would be someone else. I kept as quiet as I could and threw myself into my studies.

5

'Look! Two men holding hands!' Abbass shouted, pointing out of the window. The men wore shalwar kameez, traditional Pakistani dress and strolled down the muggy Pakistani street as if their outward affection were entirely normal. 'Friends do that here,' my dad said. I couldn't understand how something so unacceptable at home caused not even a blink here. The sound of intermittent car horns mingled with the Lahore wind and dust. From the back seat I watched a different world swish by. I was thirteen and had only caught glimpses of Pakistan in photos until then. The unfinished roads were bumpy and with each jolt my attention was drawn to another part of the alien landscape. Overcrowded rickshaws and colourfully painted lorries ferrying vegetables I didn't recognise. People transporting goods by donkeys attached to wooden carts. This is what Mum and Dad meant when they spoke of home, a place that was until then intangible to me but deeply real to them. A place where everyone looked like us. One in which we were no longer the exception, we were the rule.

'Mine looks a bit like this one,' my cousin Saima said, flicking through pages of *Asian Wedding* magazine. She was marrying one of our other cousins in a few days. We sat on her bed, surrounded by clothes, jewellery and magazines.

'I like the white one,' I said, pointing to one of the pictures.

'Yeah me too but I didn't want them all thinking I'm trying to be too Western, you know?' As she turned the pages I stared at the models. The women wore intricately stitched and colourful saris. The men stood tall in sherwanis, plain knee-length jackets with Nehru collars, slim trousers and flat shoes that tended to curl at the ends like those of Aladdin's genie. The majority of the models were white. Not just fair-skinned but actually white people dressed in our clothes. In the bathrooms of several relatives, I'd seen skin-whitening cream and used some on my face. In my culture it seemed that behaving too white came with a stigma that looking too white did not.

'Wait, you haven't seen it yet, right?' Saima said, placing the magazine in front of her on the bed.

'Seen what?' I asked.

'*East is East* – everyone's talking about it. We have to watch it.'

The film had caused a stir in the British Pakistani community. It told the story of a 1970s working-class, half-English half-Pakistani family growing up in a terraced house in the north of England. Pakistani parents hated it because it was the realisation of their deepest fears – despite the protagonist father's best efforts, the children were ambivalent about their Muslim heritage, wanting instead to be English.

The opening scene showed us the wedding of the eldest son, Nazir. Saima gave me a nudge of excitement, a nod to her own impending wedding day. Nazir looked visibly nervous, which was unsurprising given he hadn't yet met his bride. His dad, played by Om Puri, placed a golden hat on Nazir's head, with gold tinsel which dangled over his anguished face. Om Puri was every Pakistani father. He had a moustache, spoke imperfect English, complained about Indians and insisted on going to the mosque. Nazir sat on a stage in an old Yorkshire school hall, waiting for his bride to arrive.

'I'm just going to have to sit there ... it's so weird,' Saima said, referring to the tradition whereby the bride and groom sit elevated and lifeless onstage while their wedding is celebrated in front of them, mostly by people they do not know.

'If he's boring I'll keep you company.' I smiled at her.

Meanwhile, in the movie, Nazir looked at his new bride, stood up and whispered, 'I can't do this ... sorry, Dad.' He ran through the hall, pushing past the guests, and exited the wedding as his family and Saima and I looked on in disbelief. 'What's he doing?!' Saima shouted. 'She's so pretty, why doesn't he want her?' Nazir's photo was removed from the wall of the family home and the film continued, providing no explanation as to why he'd abandoned his nuptials though later his dad confirmed that his eldest son was dead.

'Dead?' Saima asked.

'Maybe he was sick?' I suggested.

'Why would he run off if he were sick? Why wouldn't he just tell them?'

It transpired that Nazir was in fact alive and living in a different city. His younger siblings crashed the high-end shop where he worked, only to find him in flamboyant clothing, kissing a white man.

'Oh ... my ... God,' Saima gasped. I sat silent and tried to clear the lump that had formed in my throat. The film ended and, to my relief, Saima hadn't mentioned Nazir again, too caught up in her own storyline by then. As we prepared for the mehndi, the traditional henna celebration, taking place the following day, my mind stayed with Nazir and the blank space on the wall where his portrait once sat.

The outside of my auntie's house was decorated in fairy lights for the night of the mehndi, a thousand golden raindrops hanging from the first-floor balcony. Inside, the white marble living-room floor was scattered with pink rose petals, while the banisters of the marble staircase that swept up one side of the living room were wrapped in garlands of bright yellow marigolds. I was only thirteen but could already imagine the night of my own mehndi: I could imagine my bride, so excited to celebrate a moment she had been preparing for all her life. And me, eager to take this step into Pakistani manhood, surrounded by family.

Amid the noise of clapping and cheering, Panjabi MC's 'Mundian To Bach Ke' suddenly blasted from downstairs. I knew it was Abbass. He loved that song and would ooze confidence when he danced, encircled by the family, all of whom loved him for his easy manner and fat cheeks.

'Go and see what's going on,' Saima ordered as she moved to the beat. She resented having to wait for her grand entrance, I could tell. I ran downstairs, expecting to see Abbass throwing arms in the air mid-squat, with aunties and uncles throwing money at him as he bounced up and down. I paused before entering the room. They'd expect me to join in, dance like Abbass, charm them with a charisma that only he had. I was awkward and struggled to find ways to endear myself to them so I waited behind the marigolds.

Abbass was there in the circle but he wasn't dancing, he was hiding. Hiding behind one aunt and then an uncle and then another aunt, as they giggled at his misfortune. He was trying to dodge the flamboyant dancer intent on pursuing him. It was a man. No, a woman. It was a person dressed in women's clothes, with effeminate movements but a masculine face, a hijra. Hijras were transgender or intersex Pakistanis who lived beyond the margins of society, on its streets and in its alleyways. Thrown out by their families and not welcome anywhere else. Except here, for a few hours. During the day they made money dancing at weddings and at night they made money selling their bodies to married men.

She had short hair for a woman, long hair for a man. She was too thin, almost malnourished. She wore a blue shalwar kameez with a pink shawl. The shawl kept falling off her shoulders as she danced around the room, collecting the notes that had been thrown at her feet by the guests. I noticed she was sweating and imagined interrupting the performance to offer her a glass of water. I'd never seen a hijra before and neither had Abbass. My auntie's husband told us they were devil creatures but my auntie insisted that we should pity them and that inviting them to perform brought blessings on the house. I wondered what blessings could come from this humiliation. I missed Walthamstow suddenly. I no longer wanted to be in Pakistan. I wanted my school, my mosque, my home.

As my extended family clapped with enthusiasm, I tried to look away but something compelled me to watch. Each shake of her hip and whip of her neck made me feel as cold as the marble staircase on which I sat.

6

Family planning was not my parents' forte. I was born before the first anniversary of their marriage, and Abbass ten and a half months later. My dad wasn't in the room when either of us came into the world, a door stood between him and my mum's screams. The birthing room was no place for a man, he told me on a hot 1998 August day as we waited outside for the arrival of my new sibling.

For me and Abbass, at the ages of thirteen and twelve, my new brother, Raza, was the ultimate plaything. For my parents, it was a tense time. Raza was the catalyst for a series of unpredictable arguments and the near collapse of their relationship.

My mum was still working as a primary-school teacher and, since his return from Pakistan, my dad had licensed a post office franchise not far from Walthamstow. They both worked long hours, but, like many women, my mum's day didn't end when she came home. My dad and I sat in the kitchen watching my mum make rotis. She mentioned in passing that she was tired and I felt guilty that she was having to feed us. As she sprinkled flour onto the large chopping board, I offered to help.

'No, no, you can't make rotis,' my dad said meaning *you*, a boy. 'No son of mine will make rotis.'

'But why not? I don't mind,' I said.

'No, no, Mochie. You must focus on your studies. Work hard and get me a cook one day when you are a rich lawyer, OK?' my mum said. I thought about how lucky it was that I didn't have a sister because she would have been treated differently to her brothers. I would have been sat watching TV while she helped Mum, whether she wanted to or not. Dad had once said we would have moved back to Pakistan because he wouldn't raise a daughter here.

Not long after, I was home alone and I had turned on the TV to find a blonde girl dressed in school uniform, gyrating in a classroom. The music was infectious.

'*Don't you know I still believe that you will be here and give me a siiiiiiggggggnnnnnn,*' I screeched, safe in the knowledge that only my drug-dealer neighbours might hear. I was less worried about what they would think than my parents.

'*Hit me baby one more …*' Midway through the song – by now I was throwing both arms wildly around – my dad entered the room. From the look of fury on his face, I could tell he had been lurking outside for some time. Abruptly I stopped dancing, and turned to face him as Britney continued to shake her stuff in the background.

I wondered whether he might grab the remote and hurl it at me. He raised his hand and pointed at me. 'You will not do things like this again, do you hear me?'

'Yes, Daddy,' I said hastily, wishing I could stare at the ground instead, but I was locked into his gaze. This incident might have festered between us had it not been for his leaving us once more.

The night before Eid that year, I was filled with anticipation. My mum had been preparing food for days. Kebabs, chicken on skewers, and my favourite desserts, sweet vermicelli *seviyan* and mangoes. In her local town in Pakistan, my mum had been the mango-eating champion. 'It's not Eid without mangoes,' she insisted.

On the day of Eid, eating before the women didn't seem right seeing as they had cooked everything but I kept my thoughts to myself. After I'd stuffed myself with as much *seviyan* as I could manage, I went outside to play in the street as the guests started to thin out. I cycled up and down the narrow pavement, forbidden to go any further. As I cycled towards the house, I could hear the rumblings of a row. I jumped off my bike, dragged it inside and ran into the living room.

Usually I stood between my parents when they were rowing, to make sure they didn't hurt each other, but I never screamed. Although their voices were raised, it would have been disrespectful, disobedient for me to do the same. But this time I did. I yelled at them to stop; it was Eid, a holy day.

The ensuing ceasefire lasted only a few days and soon my dad was packing his bags again. He visited us regularly but no longer lived at home. His relatives came over to talk things through with my mum but left abruptly after she refused to take full responsibility for the conflict. I didn't really grasp the source of tension between them but I knew it couldn't only be her fault. It seemed, however, that people were going to blame her for leaving her three sons fatherless. The onus was on her to resolve things.

'Mochie, sit here,' she said as we prepared for bed one evening. She was subdued and I could tell that the fighting had worn her down. 'They are all blaming me and it isn't fair. They are saying that my decisions will have a negative impact on you and your brothers, but you have to promise me ...' She paused to contain her emotions. 'You are the eldest and your brothers look up to you. You have to promise me that you will make a success of yourself, get us out of here and prove that we don't need them. OK, my son?' Although I couldn't see the war, her words resonated like a battle cry. I was only fourteen but it felt like she now expected me to be a man.

'I ... I promise, Ami, I promise.' My reply as sincere as my anxiety.

In her more vulnerable moments my mum blamed herself for the break-up of our home. When her thoughts were less coherent, she became convinced that someone had put the evil eye, or *nazar*, on our family. A woman from the mosque told her to search the house for pages from the Quran that might have been burned, a sacrilegious act, and hidden there by some wrongdoer intent on casting black magic. One Saturday I helped her search behind sofas, underneath beds and inside pockets for an explanation for the turmoil. We found nothing.

I had a different worry brewing. What if my parents' separation was not black magic but a sign? If it was an evil eye that had cursed us, maybe it didn't come from someone else, but from within me.

'Let's talk about sex, ba-by, let's talk about you and me, let's talk about all the good things and the bad things that may-be, let's talk about seexxx!' Uncle Tier sang over Salt-N-Pepa as he danced in our living room, which seemed too small to contain his wide six-foot-two frame. 'This song ... don't tell your dad I let you listen to it, OK?' I nodded along. Pakistani families did not talk to their children about relationships. When lips threatened to meet on screen there was a collective violent scramble for the remote control and sex wasn't even in the vocabulary.

Uncle Tier was more real to me than anyone else. His unapologetic love of music and dancing seemed brave. Abbass and he shared a birthday, a middle name and a passion for Arsenal. More than that, though, they shared an affable nature I couldn't emulate. I was an awkward teenager, constantly second-guessing my behaviour. They radiated an effortless magnetism. What Uncle Tier and I did share, though, was a love of music.

'He is the man! Listen to this,' he said excitedly as George Michael's video for 'Fast Love' played. He could see my admiration for his hero. 'Did you like that?' he asked, his big brown eyes enthusiastically waiting for the green light to play another of George's *bangers*, 'Too Funky'. The songs oozed a wet, leather sensuality.

'Turn it down, Tier!' my mum shouted, appearing from the kitchen. He stopped dancing to look at her, his face serious.

'I still can't believe it, Rube,' my uncle said, suddenly subdued. Rube was his nickname for her.

'So what happened again?' Mum asked.

'He was getting his knob off with some undercover policeman in a loo,' he said. My mum giggled.

'Well, he shouldn't be doing that, should he, and especially not in a public toilet!' she said, more instinctively than disapprovingly.

'Oh, come on, Rube. It doesn't seem fair to entrap someone like that. I don't care what he is, George is still my man!' he exclaimed.

'What does lewd act mean, Ami?' I asked. Slightly alarmed by the question, she replied simply, 'Something haram, Mochie. Something Allah does not like.' I knew from the story that whatever had happened, it had happened with another man and a blurry discomfort was slowly coming into focus.

Watching TV presenter Johnny Vaughan shout 'you beauty' and stroke his cheeks at pictures of men with huge sideburns was the highlight of my morning before I went to school, especially because, at the time, I was willing the bum fluff on my fourteen-year-old face to grow. One day, as I awaited the latest parade of facial hair, a close-up appeared of a young actor called Charlie Hunnam. The image caused a small sensation in my gut. His shaggy blond hair fell over his forehead, his blue eyes beamed, and with his soft pink lips he spoke about a TV show he was in. I was transfixed by the beauty spot on his face, it moved as he spoke; I was sure I had never seen anyone more perfect. The programme cut to a clip of him, topless. I could feel the half-eaten bits of cereal drop from my gawping mouth. He lay on a bed, his body hairless and lean and his white skin taut. I didn't want to blink. An older-looking man appeared on top of him and as their faces drew closer, I realised they were naked and immediately turned off the TV.

In the car with my family a few days later I spotted him. The blond boy from *The Big Breakfast* TV show. He stood four metres tall, and behind him the words *Queer as Folk*. My eyes surreptitiously followed his beaming smile and bright red T-shirt. Tuesday, 10.30 p.m., Channel 4, the billboard told me.

With only one TV in the house, I was sure I wouldn't be able to watch it, but something willed me to try. Another voice urged me not to but it had been silenced by the image of the topless blond. While my family eased into the last hours of the day I casually mentioned how awake I felt and said I might go down to watch TV for a while, anxious that 10.30 was fast approaching.

Our remote control had a 'last channel' button which allowed you to skip from Channel 4 to Channel 10 without passing through the others in sequence. Sat on the floor, propped against our beige-patterned sofa, I considered it my safety valve. I'd keep my finger firmly on the button in case anyone came downstairs. If, for some reason, they flicked through the channels, I'd be nowhere near Channel 4. Once the programme began, my senses heightened; it was as though I was descending a rocky cliff face and could slip at any moment. Within the first few minutes two men were kissing inside a phone box. The sight of it made me jump and, hitting 'last channel', an American talk show appeared. I told myself to stop. This was enough. A wave of guilt washed over me and I paused for a few minutes.

Turn off the TV and go upstairs, Mohsin. Turn it off now. Go upstairs. I was paralysed by guilt and indecision. I pressed the button again and was returned to the men from the billboard. They were lying naked on a bed, the older man astride the younger, bodies moving. The scene was mesmerising. My breath was shallow; although my mind raced I felt like I was watching it in slow motion. I couldn't see how two men would have sex. Did one penetrate the other's urethra? I really hoped not. I heard someone coming and rushed for the last channel button as if my life depended on it.

My mum walked in. 'Mochie, it's late, what are you doing?' Had she seen what I had seen? She couldn't have. Or had I been too engrossed to notice?

'I'm tired now, Ami, I'll go to bed.' I got up, expecting her to follow me out of the room, but she perched on the edge of the sofa and took hold of the remote. Instead of flicking up and down she pressed 'last channel'. I thought I would be sick. It cut to the characters now clothed and running down a hospital corridor. She watched for a few minutes. Those minutes felt like the slowest I had ever lived. Then she turned the TV off, walking past me and up to bed.

Abbass slept soundly. My mind replayed the scene over and over, trying to recall her reactions. Had she realised something that I had only just pieced together myself? I thought my *otherness* lay in the way

I spoke, the way I worked hard at school. But it was more than that. It was about the eye contact I made with a boy in class. It was in my admiration of the blond boy I had just seen on TV. It was in the distance I felt when the boys talked about the girls.

Go on, Mohsin. Say it. It's time. *I ... I'm ... I ... I'm g-gay*, I said to myself. I was overcome with a rush of exhilaration while the fluttering emotions in my chest searched frantically for a place to settle. I said it loud enough to make it real but so softly it didn't touch the walls, or the carpet or the bed. I didn't want it to tarnish the room. Saying the words made me feel like I'd been released from the dark pit of my imagination, allowed for a moment to stretch and scream. I let myself imagine him. A man who might love me, who might hold my hand one day. That was enough, just to picture him, for a brief moment.

The relief was short-lived. What would I do? I would do nothing. I could feel the angels on my shoulders scribbling furiously. I would tell no one. I would work hard, get a job, find a wife and have children just the way Allah had planned. I could never tell anyone my secret. I found the dark pit this emotion had emerged from and folded the feeling, and myself, back inside. I felt the stone-cold lid shut me in; this was a familiar darkness. A darkness that comforted my eyes after the blinding light.

7

A few months later, my dad came home. His children needed a father, he explained. Although the arguing erupted sporadically, it had mellowed, turning into an exchange between acquaintances rather than enemies.

When I got 98 per cent in a maths test, my teacher wrote to my parents telling them I had the highest score in the year by a considerable margin and that this performance was not out of the ordinary for me.

'What happened to the other 2 per cent?' my dad asked. I couldn't tell if he was joking. I knew now that there was something very wrong with me and this made getting everything else right more important.

At home, the 2 per cent let me down but at school it was the 98 per cent. Over lunch I sometimes had nowhere to sit without it being obvious that I had no one to sit with, so I began volunteering at the school library. Asian 'rude boy' culture demanded I walk as if I had a funny leg and wear my jeans below my bum, but above all, I was expected to treat my school-work with, at best, indifference. My innate desire to do well at school made me stand out and my feeble attempts at rude-boy slang only made my differences more pronounced. A lot of my school's pupils were Pakistani Muslims like me, but they sounded different. Although we were all born here, only I sounded English. I resented my voice because of the torment it invited. I walked through the brutalist school corridors with slouched shoulders and head down to try and make myself smaller, less of a target, less like a person with feelings to hurt and bones to be broken. When I had to speak in class, I did so carefully, so as to appear less intellectually curious. At times I wanted more than anything to be small enough not to exist at all, for existence seemed pointless when lived in the shadows. I preferred verbal abuse to the physical but often wondered whether the punches would have less of a lasting effect than the insults. Bruises healed, but words raided my cupboard of self-esteem, and now, three years into my school career, it was almost bare.

'Move out ma way, you fuckin' dik,' a guy said to me in the corridor. I did as I was told, aware of Abbass further along the corridor who had joined the school a year after me. My brother's expression was strained. I smiled, pretending nothing was wrong. I was ashamed of myself in his presence. An older sibling is meant to make the younger feel safe. My presence had the opposite effect. It made him vulnerable by association, and because I knew he couldn't stay silent, couldn't submit to it the way I had, I began to avoid him in school. I kept an eye out for him, and when I spotted his blue jacket, I turned the other way.

'I know what you are doing,' he said one evening at home. 'You don't have to avoid me.'

'Yes I do.'

'No you –'

'YES I DO!' I insisted, and then added, 'It's the only way I can protect you.'

Annually, the school awarded a prize for the Student of the Year. In my first year at the school, I was devastated when I was runner-up. By my fourth year, at the age of fifteen and at the start of a new millennium, I was devastated to be announced as the winner.

The next morning, I walked through the school gates, clutching the straps of my rucksack more tightly. Head down, I avoided the lines of the pavement. I told myself that if I could avoid stepping on the lines I would avoid stepping on the nerves of my bullies. As I walked towards class the verbal taunts were muffled by the sounds of punches and kicks as they landed. I tried to forget them, but these beatings were stamped on my memory in the same way the bullies had stamped on my legs. They joined the memories of 'birthday beats', the opposite of what you should give someone on their birthday.

In the first class of the day, things only got worse. 'Bof, did you win dik of da year cos you talk lyk white man?' Marlon asked in maths class as soon as the teacher stepped out. For years now Marlon had called me boffin and it had not only caught on but established its own shortened version, 'bof'. His constant jibes were like a nasty song that played on repeat, a tune which had once made my insides shrivel but had morphed into the soundtrack to my life in this school. The whole class fell silent as he asked his questions, interested more in the drama than the reply. I knew that Marlon and his gang had been hoping I would win.

I looked at him, pinned against the wall by the question. I said nothing. To say something would be to play his game. Instead, I wanted to ask why he spoke the way he did. Why they all spoke that way. Why, when it wasn't English, when it wasn't in the books we read or in the shows we watched. It wasn't from our parents or from their homelands. The words magnified our otherness as we uttered them. Making us seem more stupid. And yet, here he was. Asking me why I spoke like 'dat'.

'Seriously, dough, wyee?' Still I said nothing, my eyes fixed on his. All others fixed on me. I waited for his punch. From experience I knew they felt like a concrete slab falling on my chest. On one occasion it had knocked the air from my lungs, causing me to collapse in the playground. Word had quickly reached Abbass. He was the first person I thought of when these things happened, followed by my mum and dad.

'Is it cos you're a batty man?' he asked, pushing me to react to justify the beating that would follow. The classroom seemed frozen. My pulse raced as I imagined pulling out a gun.

'Fuck you, Marlon!' Shots fired. I wasn't quite sure where the words came from but I couldn't stop myself. His eyes widened, lips twisting as he moved in. Our maths teacher, a soft, small woman with glasses too big for her face and cardigans too big for her frame, walked back in just in time to intervene but I knew it wasn't over. It was never over.

As the bell sounded I quickly packed up, hoping I had left the incident behind, knowing I had not. Turning the corner into the science corridor, I was slammed against a door. Marlon and a friend of his blocked my path. I stood waiting for the inevitable show of aggression but something was different. Instead of quivering my muscles were tense, a rod of anger straightening them. The feeling filled me, making me a little taller.

'I'm getting vexed now, you know,' Marlon said, fist clenched. He was using a Shakespearean word that had become slang for angry but it wasn't slang at all. It was totally the correct use. This thought flashed through my mind and I wondered what he might say if I shared it with him.

'If you are going to punch me can you please hurry up because I'm late for class?' I said, drawing in slow and steady breaths. Their faces searched without success for fear in mine. Marlon's friend stepped aside. A small sense of pride found its way into the ball of anxiety that was now as much a part of my school attire as my pencil case. I hated being Student of the Year and I hated the school and I hated Marlon and I hated my life. Abuse came not just from Marlon but from the walls of toilets that spoke my name. From the sports teacher endearing himself by humiliating the weaker boys. From a group of girls I had outperformed in a meaningless reading competition. Classmates calling me a coconut (brown on the outside but white on the inside) because I spoke like I was on the BBC. One Pakistani boy looked confused when I replied in Urdu that he was a donkey's dick who had no right to call me a coconut while he couldn't understand what I was saying. I didn't translate.

I had very few friends and towards the end of my time at the school it felt like only one really cared about me. Musa's family was Pakistani too. It was difficult for him to be associated with me. If you're standing next to a target, some of the shots hit you, but Musa managed to stand right next to me and yet avoid becoming a human piñata. This was partly thanks to his unassuming manner, but more so the decency that radiated from him, warming even the coldest of thuggish hearts. It was this decency that made it easy for him to see I wasn't just a bookworm.

Although bullying crossed racial lines, gangs were divided by skin colour. In our area, if the boys let go of that divide, there was little else for them to care about. A fight between a black boy and a Pakistani boy when we were eleven, in our first school year, grew into a tornado that sucked in more and more kids, feeding off an abundance of mutual resentment that had crawled into the air.

Four years later and, during one lunchtime, Musa and I stood in the local kebab shop and looked on as a Pakistani boy was stabbed in the leg by a black outsider, who ran off as swiftly as he'd used his blade. It was apparently retaliation for a previous stabbing and I instantly imagined the end of this escalating conflict. All of us having knifed each other with only the kids with something to live for left standing.

The boy hobbled through the glass door and took a seat in the shop. I watched the blood pour down his leg. He held a bloody shirt to his wound and shouted words of revenge as we ordered double kebab rolls with chilli sauce and salad.

The stabbing led to whispers of retribution. The black kids in my year had started walking home together, afraid of being caught alone. There was a rumour that a group of Pakistani boys from outside the school might be waiting in a van parked on the route the black boys took home. Predators waiting to pounce on their prey.

Musa and I found a safe vantage point from which to watch. I had become one of the silent spectators I loathed. Around ten black kids, including Marlon, walked away from the school gates towards us and the trap. The thought of a punch taking the air out of Marlon's lungs gave me a satisfying if uneasy thrill.

As Marlon and his group walked past the plain white van on the street, several boys exploded from the vehicle onto the pavement. Each wore a sinister-looking white mask to hide their brown faces. They brandished baseball bats that, by the look of them, had already had some use. Some of the black boys ran but most fell over and were given a relentless beating. The bats ploughed into their young bodies as if into mud. It had looked as though Marlon had run off but then I saw his jacket on the ground. I recognised it because he had once used it to try and suffocate me. I spotted him, clasping his ankle. Although he must have hobbled away from the epicentre of the violence, he was still within its grasp and was struggling to stand. He tried to run but fell and let out a sharp cry. In that moment I felt his vulnerability. I hated him but I also hated seeing him like that. He looked like a scared little boy. 'We have to stop this,' I said. Musa looked at me, surprised and confused by the suggestion that there was anything we could do. A tall, masked boy with a bat spotted Marlon wriggling on the floor. As the boy approached Marlon, I felt helpless. He raised his bat, and as Marlon braced for impact I saw the fear in his face. I had fantasised about having the power to paint that expression onto him and yet seeing the ugliness of it told me it was wrong. Before the weapon made contact, calls rang out, that the police were coming. The familiar sound of sirens could be heard. Each siren brought with it a wave of relief. I drew a deep sigh as the masked attackers piled into the van and sped away. But then the black boys tried to get away too and I realised that, to them, the police meant only more trouble.

The next day in class a group of Asian boys reenacted highlights of the violence. 'Did you see Marlon get whacked? Man screamed like little bitch,' said one as the others laughed along. 'Now dey in hospital, yeah. Dey got da message, innit?' he said.

As Marlon hobbled past me some days later, it seemed disrespectful to stare at him struggling with his crutches. I avoided eye contact but, this time, through shame rather than fear. We both knew that I had looked on and done nothing. We both knew that maybe he didn't deserve my help but that I should have tried anyway.

8

In late 2000, eight years after starting Quran classes at the age of seven, I had finally finished reading the holy book and could stop the daily post-school ritual. I could now read ancient Arabic fluently, although I still had no idea what I was saying.

As a reward, my mum gave me an English copy of the Quran. I looked at the translation, with English sentences alongside the Arabic ones and felt, for the first time, as if I might find some answers.

I'd heard that the Quran told a story of the people of Sodom which made the position clear on homosexuality and I got to work on my English translation. I hoped to find scope for salvation in the text. The words were more than a thousand years old which meant that the language, albeit translated, felt like it was written in a sophisticated Shakespearean rather than in the English I knew. Much of what I read was about love and forgiveness. But then I found the section I was looking for. From what I could understand the story was about greed, lies and sexual violence. It wasn't immediately clear to me that this was about homosexuality but that's what I'd been told and I had no reason to doubt it. There it was, in black and white. The words shouting from the page. YOU ARE A TRANSGRESSING PEOPLE. They spoke of anger and fury. Every word pushed me further and deeper into a state of despair. I'd been raised to believe God loved all his creatures and I couldn't reconcile the love that Islam had given me with what was going through my mind.

Before that moment, I had felt wrong, yes, but not evil. That was Satan. It was murderers and rapists. It was evidently me too. The conviction on these pages brought it clearly into focus, making it impossible to ignore the sinful feelings inside me. I was disgusted with myself and ashamed too.

When my mum mentioned she was planning a pilgrimage to Syria to the tomb of Zaynab, the prophet's granddaughter, I insisted on joining her.

'Bhibhi Zaynab will grant you anything you ask for, son,' my dad told me as we said our goodbyes at the airport. I was counting on it. My parents' pride at my enthusiasm for the trip was excruciating.

Damascus, Syria's capital, reminded me of Lahore. Our guide was Molana Saab, a Pakistani Shia imam who had moved to Damascus to immerse himself in faith, in the shadows of the mosque of Bhibhi Zaynab. He was bearded, wore a black turban on his head and a dark brown shawl over his white floor-length shirt. His thick glasses gave his enlarged eyes a bewildered quality.

The gold-leaf roof of the dome glistened even at night. The mosque was divided by gender. I accompanied Molana Saab while my mum, nan and two-year old Raza walked round to the women's entrance. In the mosque a metal grill protected the coffin that sat directly underneath the dome. The ceiling was decorated with intricate Islamic patterns of blue, white and turquoise. Molana Saab told me that it was a place of miracles, that anything I asked for would be granted. Allah was in the room. I could feel it. I was filled with a belief that felt as solid and as thick as the gold doors I had just passed through. Finding a gap in the crowds, I grabbed the grill with both hands, wrapped my fingers firmly around the metal and closed my eyes. I bowed my head and prayed, squeezing the bars until my hands hurt and then I squeezed harder still. *Allah, Bhibhi, take this away.* I couldn't bring myself to use the word 'gay' when talking to Allah or his messengers. My thoughts were desperate and incoherent. *I don't want to feel this way. I want to see my family in heaven. I want to make you proud, make my parents proud. I want to live a life without sin. Please, please, please take this away. I don't want it. Take it away. Take it away. Cure me. I beg you. Cure me please.*

I was pushed aside to make way for other pilgrims, desperate for their own miracles. I sat as close to the coffin as I could without being trodden on and purposefully immersed myself in my predicament. I knew why Allah had made me gay. To Muslims, life is a test and your behaviour determines whether you go to heaven or hell. Some are tested by poverty, others by having too much. Some by the sudden death of their children, or illness. Some by temptation. Sinful lust was my test. It was a blessing really, preferable to other possibilities. All I had to do was refrain from thought or action that defied the teachings of the Quran, and take positive steps in the opposite direction. Steps towards whomever Allah had chosen to be my wife.

It came to me with the force of an epiphany. I would find a girlfriend. I thanked Bhibhi Zaynab for listening to me. For hearing my prayers and for helping me find a way through. As I left the mosque, making my way onto the courtyard's moonlit floor, my nan asked me what I had prayed for. It was the most obvious question for which I had not prepared an answer. I considered explaining to her that to tell her would break the spell, in much the same way you keep your birthday wish a secret after you have blown out the candles. When she wouldn't let it go, I told her I had asked Allah to find me a good wife. She told me that if he didn't, she would.

*

Once back at home, I considered how to put my plan to get a girlfriend into action. My parents never spoke to me about puberty or the birds and the bees. Or girls. Sitting me down to discuss dating would be like sitting me down to discuss the wrongs of stealing. It was unnecessary because it was obviously something we did not do. This made it easy to hide from them my lack of attraction to girls. It also helped me hide my efforts to find a girlfriend.

Having a girlfriend would undermine my family's honour, their *izzat*. Faith and *izzat* are not the same thing but, much like two languages with a shared history, they have a complex relationship with one another. Although I feared the community humiliation my parents might face if it transpired I had a girlfriend, it was a risk worth taking and one that, perversely, would pay off were it uncovered.

Yasmin was Muslim, of course, and it all started more by fortuitous accident than anything I could conjure up. She was a popular, pretty girl in the year above. Her light skin, petite build and captivating smile made her one of the most desired girls in school. Bollywood had just released *Mohabbatein*, a blockbuster about six teenagers trying to find relationships at their Indian boarding school. Bollywood struck a chord with the kids at my school where Hollywood did not. There was no suggestion of sex; instead the story centred on controlling parents and cultural expectations and, crucially, the characters were played by people that looked like us, albeit more glamorous. Not having an identifiable crush in the midst of the hysteria whipped up by the film might invite unwelcome scrutiny. I assumed, when asked who my crush was, that by naming Yasmin I was safe. She would never know and, even if she did, I was the year below and she was out of my league. She was the perfect decoy. Perfect until someone decided to play cupid, informing her of my fictitious affections.

The following day, I was told she wanted to meet. I agreed reluctantly. At the meeting, on the hilly field adjacent to the school car park, she said she wanted us to get to know each other but I wasn't sure there was anything interesting about me. I had made a list of things I could revert to at even the hint of an awkward silence. 1) Teachers we had in common. 2) Her dad's shop and my dad's post office. 3) Her GCSEs. 4) Was she watching *Big Brother*? (I really liked the Irish guy but wouldn't tell her he was my favourite because of his accent.) 5) Did she think Tupac was still alive?

Amongst my nerves my list became jumbled and incoherent and I made my excuses and hurried home. It was an uncomfortable thirty minutes. I struggled to make eye contact, looking up only occasionally to find her big eyes peering at mine, too close to avoid.

A few days passed before one of her friends sent a message on her behalf.

Yasmin wants to meet you tonight after school.

OK, I wrote, not knowing what else to say.

We met again on the same hilly field.

'So aren't you going to ask me?' Yasmin said. My fifteen-year-old mind was blank.

'Erm … ask you what?'

'Aren't you going to ask me out?' The question caught me off guard.

'Oh … well … will you … will you go out with me?' I cringed on the inside as I said the words. Instinctively, I could tell it was the wrong thing to do but what other option did I have? I had formulated this plan, built this structure and now I had to stand on it, even though I felt like it would inevitably topple.

'You have a girlfriend.' Abbass cornered me when I got home with what didn't appear to be a question.

'What?' I didn't know what to say.

'The whole school is talking about it. Why didn't you tell me?' He looked hurt. He wanted to know why he'd heard it through the grapevine rather than from me. He wanted an explanation for the distance it marked between us. I hated lying to him so I said nothing.

Yasmin and I met after school three days in a row. At the weekend she added me on MSN Messenger and insisted we chat on Saturday evening, during which she told me how much she liked me.

By Monday my guilt was overwhelming. I was using her as nothing more than a prop in my own story and it was unkind. After school, she asked me to walk her home and I obliged. On the way, without forewarning, she took my hand and smiled kindly at me. Nothing about it felt right. Alarm bells rang in my head and my stomach clenched.

That evening, over MSN Messenger, I told her that my auntie had spotted us holding hands and called my parents. That my parents had forced me to break it off and so I couldn't go out with her any more. I wasn't sure whether she believed me but in that moment it didn't matter. Saying it in person made it real but from behind the safety of a computer screen I was blind to her reaction and so felt liberated from accountability for it, as though I was absolved of responsibility because I hadn't spoken the words out loud, hadn't seen her tears for myself.

The initial flood of relief I felt was soon stifled by a new rumour. 'Mohsin, Yasmin's friends are talking about you,' a classmate told me. I hadn't anticipated this. That by being with her for only three days before breaking it off I would raise rather than bury questions over my sexuality.

'Go on,' I said.

'It isn't very nice.'

'Just tell me.'

'Well, they're telling everyone that you must be ...'

'Must be what?' I said, panicked.

'... frigid.'

Perfect. I wanted to laugh. Frigid I could handle.

But it wasn't perfect, because my attempts to bring myself closer to Allah's teachings had failed spectacularly. I'd lasted three days and a single session of heterosexual hand-holding before running for the exit.

9

While my own schooldays were approaching an inglorious end, Abbass was, by this point, on both the cricket and football teams. He spoke like everyone else, which raised even more questions about why I sounded the way I did. The distance in our social standing at school created one at home. I blamed him, adamant that he was embarrassed by me, but, in truth, I was embarrassed by myself. We went days without speaking, the silence broken by sudden and aggressive verbal spats. I moved into the computer room downstairs to get as far away from my family as I could. It didn't feel far enough, although the dial-up Internet we had installed a few months earlier allowed me to see the world beyond my bedroom.

Musa was computer-literate, so I asked him to teach me how to surf the Web, beyond MSN Messenger.

'Watch this,' he said. We were in his bedroom; he had his own computer.

'Basically it's like MSN, but instead of messaging your friends, you can message random people anywhere. There are loads of different chat rooms. Look, this one is for sex ...'

'To have sex with people?' I asked, my voice snagged on the word *sex*.

'No, man! Just typing sexy stuff, innit? Watch.' He still hadn't taken his eyes away from the screen and neither had I. We messaged users whose names sounded vaguely feminine, asking them about their boobs and sniggering at our collective mischief.

Later that night, I waited until everyone was asleep before turning on the computer. Its glaring light illuminated only me and the keyboard in the otherwise dark room. The sound of the dial tone was deafening. After a pause to make sure no one was stirring upstairs I followed Musa's instructions to get back onto the chat-room site. First I had to pick a username.

'M.U.S.A.16,' I typed out. Next I had to select from a list of chat rooms.

JUST SEX. That was the site we'd been on earlier.

BDSM. That didn't sound especially gay.

LGB. No idea.

CHAT FRIENDS. Who would come on here to find friends? I thought mockingly before realising I might.

GAY. The word I'd been looking for. I entered the room and the main chat window said *Musa16 has joined the group.*

'*Hi, Musa,*' came the first message from Strokeaway.

'*Wat u lookin 4?*' wrote Bigdick567.

I didn't know what I was looking for. Why was I on here at all? I closed the window. A minute and a few deep breaths later, I reconnected.

Musa16 has joined the group.

'*No Paki time-wasters,*' read the message immediately beneath it from Bigdick567. How could he tell I was Pakistani? I wondered.

'*Sht da fk up u dumb prick,*' wrote Bollywoodboy23. I watched the screen as they argued, thousands of miles away and apart. They were exchanging messages of little consequence that would be forgotten even faster than the time it took to read them, but it was captivating. A private message popped up from Bollywoodboy23.

'*Fuk him. Diks like dat on here all da time. Hows u?*'

I looked down at the keyboard, not sure whether to type or hit myself over the head with it.

'*Hi ... are you Indian?*' I wrote.

'*Haha u dnt waste time! Yeah, u?*'

'*Turns out the dumb prick isn't so dumb after all, I'm Pakistani. Haha,*' I wrote.

'*Haha ... where u from?*'

'*London ... u?*'

'*Canada.*'

There was a pause while I waited for him to say something else.

'*So, do your parents know about you?*' I typed out all the letters. It seemed rude to ask the question at all, but even more so to do it without going to the effort of using the correct spelling. He didn't reply. I watched closely but he wasn't active on the main group either. I waited, needing to know that I wasn't alone.

'*Nah ... complicated. Dey want me 2 marry my cuz in India ... Asian parents such a stress haha.*'

'*Have you thought about telling them?*' By hiding behind an online mask, I was able to take off the one I used for the real world.

'*U mad?! Dey wud kill me.*'

'*My parents would kill me too. I'll never tell them either. Can I have your email?*' I hit send before my sense got the better of me. I waited for a reply, staring at the little box with his name in the title bar, willing for an email address to appear. I wanted that email address more than I'd ever wanted anything, as if having it was proof I wasn't all by myself. After a few minutes I added: '*Maybe we could be friends? :)*' I regretted the smiley face. After failing to respond for ten minutes, the title bar blinked. I rushed my mouse to it.

Bollywoodboy23 has left the conversation, it read.

*

On the Monday of the last week of school, year 11s started ceremonially signing each other's white shirts. I accepted the few requests I got to sign people's shirts but I didn't want my own signed. It was a popularity contest I knew I would lose. The reality was I might end up with insults on my back and I wasn't going to let them etch those into my clothes as well as my mind. I daydreamed of scenes from US high school films. The teen drama *She's All That* was set in a school with beautiful Californian kids. Its resident geek was transformed into a popular, good-looking albeit unlikely prom queen. As the film's theme song, 'Kiss Me', buzzed in my head, I imagined Freddie Prinze Jr, the lead actor, coming into school and sweeping me off my feet, as my classmates sang along in the background. Although the bubble of that dream quickly burst, school was almost over and I *was* excited. Excited to get away from Marlon and the others and excited to see what came next.

First thing the next morning, we were told that a special assembly had been called by our head of year and that we should make our way to the sports hall. The hall had a dark green floor and three-storey-high ceilings. The painted lines to mark the basketball and badminton areas had faded with age. The humming sound of extractor fans reminded me of the mock GCSEs I'd taken in this hall recently, in the run-up to the real ones that were fast approaching. In the presence of year 11 tutors and around 180 students, our head of year spoke of the importance of the exams we were about to take and how our lives started after they finished. He spoke fondly of memories from school trips and recounted anecdotes of interactions between the teachers and the popular kids. He told us that the school would always be a part of who we were and that we would always be a part of it. He then explained that the reason this sounded like a goodbye is because it was. The start of exam leave and our last day at school would not be Thursday, as we'd been told, but today. To circumvent gang violence on the final day, they surprised us by moving our leave date forward, to that very moment.

Before there was time to be surprised, disappointed, or angry at the teachers for this abrupt ending, we were herded to the fire exit in the far corner, leading out to a local car park, and cut loose into the world. As the mostly black and brown sixteen-year-olds turned our backs to the school that had raised us, in the car park we were greeted by police officers. So this was the first day of the rest of our lives. A trap. We were stopped and searched by white officers who looked for weapons that we might use to hurt each other.

Initially I looked on with satisfaction when I saw Marlon being searched. But the tired frustration in his eyes as he rolled them made me wonder how often he was humiliated in this way. I might not have liked him, but I wasn't sure he deserved to be treated like a criminal. Then they started searching Musa. And then they stopped another boy from my year and patted down another. It was as if we were going through aggressive airport security before being allowed to start our lives. Passers-by stared at the spectacle, unsurprised by what they saw. I protested only meekly. I had something to say about the unfairness of it all but no words with which to say it. My voice had run scared. I felt ashamed for myself, for Musa, even for Marlon. For the fact that this was going to be the memory of our last day at school.

10

'Just apply and see what happens.'

'But, Mum, I don't want to go there.'

'Well, it's not a choice yet, is it, Mochie? Why don't you just apply and if you decide you don't want to go, you don't have to? But at least try. Have a look around.'

The local college, Leyton Sixth Form, required a minimum of five A–Es at GCSE. Although it was where I wanted to go, it wasn't where I would be going if my grades were good enough. My mum still had her eye on the grammar school, the same one I had tried, years earlier, to get into.

My English teacher agreed to help me with the application to Ilford County High School. As we sat in her classroom after school, she looked through the questions and reviewed my answers. 'I think this place will be really good for you, Mohsin, you need this.' Each year they received dozens of applications for five spaces in the sixth form, and after an interview with a grey-haired deputy head teacher, I was offered a conditional place.

Once my exams were over, I had nothing to do but wait for the results, so I got a summer job. It was my first day in the menswear department of House of Fraser, tucked away on the third floor of the large department store on Oxford Street, with bright artificial lighting and endless escalators. The manager looked down and read out my name at the team meeting of around twenty sales assistants, all dressed, head to toe, in black. My awkward demeanour and ill-fitting trousers told them I was new to the job and to the outside world. 'MO-MO-MO-SHIN. Hmmm ... is that your Christian name or is it ZEEDEE? I can't tell from this form.' He had mispronounced both. I paused, struggling to decipher what he was asking me.

'Er ... I don't ... I don't have one,' I replied.

'You don't have one what?'

'I ... er ... I don't have a Christian name.' The mumbling stopped.

'What do you mean?' His eyebrows met in a frown.

'I don't ... well, er ... have a Christian name because I'm a Muslim,' I said reluctantly.

The group laughed. My unease and confusion made clear it was neither sarcasm nor political. A young Asian guy put his arm around me, smiling, and asked me my first name. After that day, I came in for eleven shifts in a row before the same manager finally explained the rota system.

On the morning of GCSE results day, my mum took a £5 note from her purse and circled it over my head three times as she said a prayer. Most mums had to stand on tiptoe to perform this religious ritual but not mine. 'You are going to do well, inshallah, my son.'

I took my envelope to an empty classroom. I wanted to be alone. To have a moment to prepare myself for the news, good or bad. I tore away the brown flap and pulled out the results slip:

A, A*, A, B, A, A*, A, B, B, A.

I felt a surge of excitement as I raced out of the school to find Mum and Dad, who were waiting, no doubt with bated breath, in the car park.

'Mohsin!' the shout came. I looked round to see my English teacher. 'Well done, you've got some of the best results the school has ever seen.'

We hugged as I thanked her for everything she had done for me. I turned to leave and saw Marlon perched on a table, a disheartened look on his face and a torn envelope by his side. 'Well done, man.' he said.

I couldn't wait any longer to show my parents the results. I had never seen such an expression of pride on their faces. It was as though the brightness of my success might make it near impossible for them to see who I really was. And for me the exhilaration of succeeding felt like a drug that briefly numbed the pain of my sexuality. We drove the short distance to Ilford County High, Bollywood tunes blasting from the car mixed with screams from Uncle Tier on the phone, where the new school confirmed I'd be starting in September.

As a reward for my results, my mum took us to New York. We stayed with her cousin in New Jersey, a fifty-minute train ride from Manhattan and a picturesque view of its skyline greeted us on the way in and waved goodbye on the way back. The Twin Towers were its centrepiece and going to the Top of the World, the viewing gallery in the south tower, was one of the first things Abbass and I did on our trip. Rather than pay to go up, Mum and Raza waited for us on the ground floor to save money.

From up here, the buildings below looked like people, different shapes and sizes bustling confidently up against one another. The view was the most magical thing I had ever seen, sparking the exhilarating anticipation of what was waiting for me out there in the world. For the first time, the clouds were almost close enough to touch.

A few days later, back in London and in our living room, my family and I stared in collective disbelief at footage of the first plane and then the second ploughing into the towers, over and over again. The tears poured down my mum's face, as she recalled waiting for her sons in the lobby of the south tower, and imagined the planes striking at that moment, unable to reach us at the top as the two buildings burned. She thought of the parents watching for whom this was actually true.

I was shaken to the core when I heard that the attack had allegedly been carried out by people who called themselves Muslims. That evening my dad sat Abbass and me down.

'You have to be very careful. The world is a dangerous place right now and we will be blamed for all of this. Your only defence is a good education. You must study hard. OK?' His words added to the sense of danger that had settled over our house.

I was miserable at having to start again at a new school, to have to try and endear myself to a new group of people, and not just people – boys. Sixteen- and seventeen-year-old boys with no female influence to dilute the laddish behaviour they expected of each other. An environment heaving with competition, and with the unwavering focus on getting into a top university.

'Which universities will you be applying to, young man?' our form tutor asked each one of us on our first day, as we sat in the chemistry lab in our dark suits and ties.

'Oxford,' said several. 'Cambridge,' said others.

'You must all be aiming for the Russell Group otherwise you are wasting your time at this school, understood?' he said.

'What about you, newbie? Which of the Russell Group have you got your eye on?' He sounded like the queen.

'I don't know,' I mumbled, not wanting to admit I didn't know what he was talking about. I could feel their eyes on me, trying to figure out whether I'd be a threat to their place in the academic pecking order. I knew that I wasn't, that I didn't belong. At my secondary school, I'd refrained from speaking for fear of being punched for saying something clever. Here I feared being ridiculed for saying something stupid. They thought carefully about themselves. They considered how the decisions they made today would impact their lives tomorrow. There was an ambition in everything they did. An ambition to which I could not relate, but which, in the wake of 9/11, seemed more important than ever.

11

My dad's post office was doing well and my mum was a successful primary-school teacher. My parents scraped together enough money to get us out of Walthamstow and into Woodford, a safer, whiter neighbourhood in the suburbs of London. We were moving up in the world, or so we thought. It soon transpired that although my parents had chosen an area with less crime, they'd also chosen the wrong side of the Central Line tracks. The part of Woodford we moved to was unwelcoming to non-whites, our neighbours were initially critical of a 'Paki family' moving in, one of them told my mum. After 9/11, Muslims were easy targets and, as teenage brown boys, Abbass and I became the objects of abuse.

'Terrorist scum,' yelled one kid from the midst of a group of teenagers. 'Go back to where you came from, Paki cunt,' shouted another.

Abbass returned one Saturday from the shops sweating and breathing hard.

'What happened?' Mum asked. I looked up from the dining table where I was studying.

'These two white boys came up to me and said some shit. They started squaring up to me and wouldn't get out of my way.'

'Oh my God! Are you OK?' Mum said, pulling Abbass into her arms. I scrutinised him for signs of injury.

'Yeah, yeah. I'm fine.' He smiled. 'But I'm not sure about them.'

'Huh?!' I exclaimed.

'So one of them comes at me and I punched him right on the nose and he took a drop,' Abbass said proudly. 'And then the other one went for me but I tripped him up too.'

'And then what?'

'And then I just came home,' he said, shrugging.

Although there were no racial tensions at Ilford County, which was about half South Asian, half white and entirely middle class, the respective racial groups still mostly seemed to stick to their own.

I chose English literature as one of my four A levels. On the first day the teacher asked each of us what books we had read over the summer, which were our favourites and which we had liked the least and why. The boys spoke eloquently and fluently, like I was learning to do, but I was not as erudite. I understood that words mattered. A painter with two colours would never be able to paint as vividly as one with twenty.

'*Ulysses* by James Joyce was my favourite. I loved its commitment to modernist experimentation,' said the boy sitting next to me.

'I haven't really read anything this summer,' I told the class, deciding it was better to answer honestly than to be caught out later. I had never been much of a reader. My parents hadn't read to us as children and it seemed a bit boring when I could play outside or watch TV instead. Reading required me to sit still, which I found difficult because my mind wandered into dangerous territory.

'Please see me afterwards,' the teacher said before swiftly moving on. At the end of the class he strongly encouraged me to drop the subject, explaining that he could only teach boys who demonstrated a commitment to literature that I clearly lacked. I took his advice and dropped English.

*

A year later, in late 2002, it was time to start applying to universities. The school did not consider me to be the right calibre for Oxbridge, which didn't offend me because neither did I. Before my first-year results arrived, I had assumed I would get Cs, or Bs if I was lucky.

'You got three As – you should at least try!' my dad insisted. 'I promise Allah that if you get in – sorry, *when* you get in – I will take you back to Syria, to our prophet's granddaughter, in thanks to him.'

'Dad, I'm not going to get in. That place is for people like Tony Blair, Bill Clinton, not people like us.'

'Imran is Pakistani, he went there, didn't he? And Benazir.'

'Yes, Dad, but they were really clever and rich.' As ever, the decision to make the application wasn't mine, but my parents'.

I chose Oxford because the application form was shorter than the one for Cambridge. I opened the prospectus and found the information on the undergraduate degree in jurisprudence. The page gave statistics on the average number of successful applicants. 12.5 per cent for jurisprudence and 8.7 per cent for jurisprudence with legal studies in Europe, which made it the most competitive undergraduate course at the university.

'Which universities in London are you looking at?' my dad asked. My parents' fixation on Oxford was strong enough to overcome their desire to keep me at home. But any mention of a college outside London, aside from Oxford, was coolly received.

'LSE, Kings, but Bristol has a great law department and Durham is meant to be really –'

'Durham? No, no, no – you will stay in London. There are plenty of good universities here.'

'So I shouldn't apply to Oxford then?'

'That's different.' His smile faded as he realised I was serious about these other universities.

'I'd like to apply at least. You and Mum are always saying apply and then see what happens.'

'Absolutely not. If you want to apply outside of London I will not stop you, but I will not support you.'

'Dad, you aren't being fair,' I said.

'Mohsin –' he tilted his head to one side – 'What makes you think I have to be fair?'

'You are a Muslim, not one of these *goreh* who leave home to go drinking. You can get a perfectly good education in London, living here and saving money.' His tone softened to take the edge off the hammer he was wielding.

'Go into the school hall and count the number of people who have successfully got a place at Oxford to study law and then come back and tell me whether you're still thinking of applying.' I did so in earnest, realising after the count that the suggestion was made mockingly. Ilford County engraved the names of its Oxbridge pupils in gold leaf in the oak-panelled school hall. My history teacher went to Oxford himself. I didn't expect him to be so discouraging when I told him I was thinking of applying.

When boys at the school received word that they had been shortlisted for an interview, they were ecstatic to have jumped the first hurdle. Apparently not many were interviewed, let alone given places. I clicked the 'my applications – status' button on the website and waited as the page slowly loaded. Next to Oxford, it read 'Invited for interview'. There was a tiny flutter of excitement in my chest, before I reminded myself that, despite achieving this step, I was a long way from winning the race. In any case, I just wasn't good enough.

During the school's mock-interview session, I was asked to explain the difference between truth and justice. I had no idea. When asked which college I would be applying to and what reasons I would give for that decision, I said I hadn't thought about it yet, not revealing that I didn't know what he meant by 'college'. The mock interviewer, a former pupil who'd recently graduated from Oxford, told me to stop nodding my head and to stop being so agreeable. He ridiculed the only way I knew how to be and I feared the same treatment, if not worse, when it came to the real thing. Applying to Oxford was a fanciful dream of my parents. After a little encouragement from Uncle Tier, who'd been put up to it by my dad, I'd decided to indulge them. 'Go for it, son, you've got nothing to lose, I know you can do it,' he'd said, with so much love in his voice I couldn't say no.

12

The cold Oxford air, at least to my urban lungs, felt fresh and rich with possibility. Of the questions I could guess the dons might ask, the one I feared most was why I had applied to Keble. The real answer was foolish. I thought you simply applied to a place called 'Oxford University'. I didn't realise it was divided into many colleges. I chose Keble because at House of Fraser I had worked with a Pakistani guy from Walthamstow, Riz, who was there now. It was the only college I'd heard of.

The old buildings and their medieval shaped arches left me in awe. The student ambassadors I met were well spoken and friendly, if a little lofty. Their hoodies bore the college coat of arms and were like uniform for an elite club. A casual item of clothing that seemed to effortlessly separate them from us. The student who showed me to my room was really handsome and I tried not to stare. I found myself hoping I might bump into him as I walked around the college. I imagined being accepted and meeting him again on my first day and maybe getting closer to him.

But that was stupid. I was allowing myself to dream in ways that I should not. I was doing this only because of my parents. I would be rejected with just a short story to tell about the three days I had spent at Oxford. But a small pang of envy would linger, my inferiority confirmed.

As I climbed the staircase, my heart raced. The stone steps had grooves down the middle, eroded over time with thousands of historical footsteps.

'Come in, Mohsin,' said a man in a crisp suit. I was in my school trousers, and immediately thought that I should have bought a proper suit for the interview or at least cleaned my scruffy black shoes before putting them on.

Inside, a young black man sat waiting.

'Just take a seat over there,' the man in the suit said, pointing to a sofa. It seemed odd to feel comforted by the fact that one of the interviewers was black but I did. It was as if my visible differences seemed to disappear.

The room was filled with books; side by side on the many shelves, lying open on the large wooden desk and in piles on the floor. The view from the window framed a pattern of the college's vivid red brick. The interviewers started by asking questions about my hobbies. I didn't know how to be formal, so I tried to be nice instead. Then they moved on to questions about the law. There were none I couldn't answer and I left the room with a smile. I hadn't got in, I was sure. My answers weren't impressive enough; they were just the first things I could think to say. But I'd not made a fool of myself and that was enough for me.

For the Christmas holidays, my mum, brothers and I went to Pakistan. My dad stayed behind because of work. We stayed at Uncle Makki's during our visit and Mariam made me feel at home. Their five-bedroom house felt more like a five-star hotel with its marble floors, crystal chandeliers and handcrafted wooden furniture. The phone rang and a collective scream summoned me to the living room where my mum held the receiver, as the others crowded around, staring at me.

'Dear Mr Zaidi,' she said. A long pause. The words were read out by my dad over the phone to my mum and then repeated once again to everyone in the room.

Her eyes were wide, her head shaking in disbelief.

'*I am pleased, on behalf of Keble College, to tell you ...*'

Another pause.

'*... that we propose to offer you a place – OH MY God!*'

'Mum, FINISH,' I said.

'I'm trying, but it's your father, he keeps crying ... OK, OK, OK ... *for admission in October 2003 to read law with European legal studies.*' She was carefully relaying my father's words. 'Mashallah!'

I had wanted to open the letter myself but it would have been un-Pakistani to insist. This didn't happen to me, it wasn't about me; it happened to us, it was about us.

My dad said he'd opened the letter as soon as he walked in but had not been able to compose himself fully enough to pick up the phone for a while. He had dropped to his knees, put his hands up in prayer and thanked Allah. It had worked. He had left behind a life, parents and friends in Pakistan for a place where he had nothing, in the hope of building a more prosperous version of himself. His life decisions vindicated by the words in that letter.

Oxford assumed you accepted the offer. It was the first place in England ever to teach law. Of course they did. The arrogance of it was intimidating. My mum clasped the phone close to her ear, holding on tightly to the gift we had just been given. Mariam stood behind her, jumping up and down.

In that room in Lahore I was reminded of the scene in *Charlie and the Chocolate Factory* when Charlie uncovers the golden ticket. That's what it felt like. A ticket. A gold-plated ticket out of our small house and into a future where we no longer relied on living hand to mouth but they, instead, relied on me; a social contract signed when I was born now coming to fruition. Across Asia it was expected that boys would support their parents through old age. And I was now the golden boy.

I sighed. As the eldest of three boys, I respected and accepted the path my culture, religion and circumstance had dictated; finishing school with the best grades I could muster, getting into an average university and getting a City job playing a supporting role to more articulate white men. A job that would help my parents find me an appropriate wife. Oxford raised the stakes of this narrative. It placed me on a pedestal whose dizzying heights would make any fall catastrophic.

I looked at Mariam and thought about how she'd be the perfect person for me to marry. She was intelligent, considerate; my parents loved her and our families would unite. Now that I was going to be an Oxford law graduate, they might seriously consider it.

My heart pounded and my mind raced. I had been awarded a prize I did not fully understand. I had been handed a key that unlocked doors as yet invisible to me, behind them things I could not comprehend. It had to be a mistake. I calculated the time in the UK and called the university.

'Hi, can I speak to someone in admissions?'

A pause.

'Hi, I've received a letter telling me I've been accepted and I just wanted to ...'

I hadn't thought about the fact that I'd have to tell them I thought it was a mistake.

'Um ... I just wanted to make sure it wasn't a mistake?'

The woman laughed kindly and said she could check for me. She took my name and confirmed. 'No, no mistake.' I could hear the smile in her voice, from thousands of miles away. She could hear mine too as I thanked her.

Phone calls were made to grandparents, aunties, uncles, cousins, family friends and then finally the remainder of my parents' mental phonebook. I spoke to one family friend in Japan, to whom I'd never spoken before, and thanked him for his good wishes. I overheard my mum on the phone telling my nan that it was Imran Khan's college. My nan didn't know Oxford but she knew Imran. Mum looked at me differently now. They all did. Like I had managed to turn water into a non-alcoholic wine.

The one person I wanted to tell was Uncle Tier. After a few rings he answered already screaming. My dad had got to him first. I was elated by his reaction.

'It's almost time for prayer, you must thank Allah for this gift,' my mum instructed. As violently as a prick to a balloon, the elation was gone. The weight of their praise grew unbearably heavy; a ton of misplaced expectations resting on my shoulders.

How could something so positive coexist with my sexuality? Prayer was only ever about one thing for me: asking for a cure. Each time I prayed, it brought me momentary hope and peace. I couldn't understand why God had given me this miracle. And then, there it was – I realised I'd been given it for a very particular reason. I would have to sacrifice this reward to demonstrate how devout I really was. Letting go of Oxford seemed like a huge price to pay but I knew what I had to do.

Now I turned to face Mecca, for the fourth time that day. I imagined myself looking directly at the Kabba, the black cube-shaped building at the centre of the Great Mosque of Mecca, the most sacred site in Islam.

'Allah, thank you for this gift. I don't want it. Please take it back. I'd rather be normal instead. Please make me better.' Maybe this was it, I thought. Maybe I could exchange one miracle for another, an eye for an eye. For the next few months, as I studied relentlessly to achieve the required grades, I also asked Allah, daily, to take away my place at Oxford in exchange for a cure for my homosexuality.

13

Dad kept his promise to Allah to take me back to Damascus if I got into Oxford. When he brought it up, I insisted that we go as soon as possible and definitely before my exams. Last time I had nothing to offer but now I could give Allah the one thing that might actually make a difference to my life: I could sacrifice the hope and opportunity that Oxford represented for something else.

'I can drop you at the hotel but I want to go and see Bhibhi Zaynab tonight, I cannot wait until tomorrow', my dad said, as soon as we stepped off the plane into the humid air of night-time Damascus.

'No, Dad, I want to come with you.'

We were met by Molana Saab outside one of the mosque's four minarets, the top of each lit with a dark green glow. We followed him into the main prayer area, where I left them and headed straight for the enclosed coffin. With both hands on the grill and my eyes open, I prayed out loud. I was overcome with a sense of possibility. This was a place of healing, Molana Saab had said so, and I knew I would be heard only if I truly believed. I repeated different versions of the same request. Take away this gift. Cure me. Make me normal.

The next day my dad had to go into the city centre to confirm our return flights. I told him I wanted to spend time in prayer. He was encouraging, obviously delighted by my devotion. Molana Saab took me to the Great Mosque of Damascus, located within the walls of the old city and one of the oldest and largest mosques in the world. A building of sixth-century Islamic architecture, with pillars, small window frames and mosaic tiling bordering a vast marble courtyard floor, it was said to be the place to which Jesus would return at the end of the world.

Molana Saab and I spent most of the morning reading prayers on a deep red carpet beneath one of the mosque's many chandeliers. I wanted to ask him about jinn and their ability to inhabit the bodies of human beings. My sinful thoughts were becoming more elaborate. As well as imagining having sex with a man, I had now also started to fantasise about sharing a life with another man. Maybe the cure I longed for required an exorcism. The idea scared me. I avoided looking in mirrors, worried I might catch a glimpse of something evil in my eyes.

'Molana Saab,' I whispered, 'can I ask you something?' I hid my trembling hands in the folds of my tunic.

'Of course you can.' He closed his prayer book and turned to me with kind eyes.

'My friend in London thinks she is possessed by a jinn,' I said. 'Is that possible in Islam?'

I had done some research myself so I knew the answer. I'd found a video of a bearded Asian man, wide-eyed, teeth clenched, screaming the words 'Burn, burning, BURN!' as an imam read prayers by his bedside. The image terrified me but it also showed me a way out.

'Hmm … well … yes we do believe it's possible, but it isn't very common. What makes your friend think she is possessed?'

'She tells me she has evil thoughts that she can't get rid of.'

'What kind of evil thoughts?' he whispered, as if he was worried others might overhear.

I couldn't tell him the truth. 'She hasn't really explained them to me … sometimes she wants to hurt people. She prays every day to get better but it isn't working. How … how can she get rid of the jinn?'

He looked unnerved. 'Mohsin, is there anything you want to tell me?'

'No! No, it's not me, I promise, Molana Saab. Honestly, I would tell you if it were.' The idea of him or anyone else picking up a scent panicked me. At that moment I could hear the rumble of thunder in the sky.

'Tell your friend she needs to ask for help.' I nodded, too afraid to say any more. Before the word 'jihad' became synonymous with violence and terror it meant something else. It represented the spiritual struggle within oneself against sin. Praying for a cure was my own private jihad.

It was the Sunday before my eighteenth birthday. I hated Sundays. Not the days so much as the evenings. It felt like the world had shut up shop and gone home, leaving you with nothing but your thoughts for company. I also hated my birthday. It served as a reminder of what I saw as my illness, a reminder that another year had passed in this state of helplessness. I stared at my hands. I had read somewhere that a person's fingerprints faded with age. Something so much a part of you, literally etched in, that diminished over time. Was there ever a more poignant reminder that the older I became, the more difficult it would be to leave my mark on the world?

On this particular January morning, a storm was brewing. As a child I believed thunder was Allah's way of telling us he was angry. The sound of it would have me running for cover under my parents' duvet, holding on to them, while reciting the Kalma prayer, with intermittent apologies for all the naughty things I might have done. While thunder didn't have quite the same effect on me at eighteen, it still made me say a prayer inside my head and automatically consider what I might have done to upset Allah.

A card was waiting for me on my bed. The message on the front read *'For your birthday, son'*. I opened it to find that my mum had handwritten my name next to each line of the message inside:

> Making his way with a mind of his own – *Mohsin*
> Making a difference and making it known – *Mohsin*
> That he has his own hopes and dreams to pursue – *Mohsin*
> Which is why, son, these wishes are special, like you.

The thought of my own hopes and dreams making me special made me cry. I didn't feel special. I felt disgusting.

I could guess from my dad's suggestion that we go shopping together for a present that at home my family was planning something. We returned to find cousins and friends waiting for us by the front door. They shouted 'Surprise!' and I pretended I was. They broke into song. I wondered what our racist neighbours would make of a large group of brown men and women with headscarves singing 'Happy Birthday' in loud, east London accents.

I didn't know how to carry myself. Nothing felt natural or right. On the surface I felt detached. Underneath was a restless agitation. I had chained my sexuality to a post and it was barking loudly to be set free. I felt tired. Not tired, exhausted. I didn't want to be here, among all these people. I was lying, indulging everyone in the façade of being the perfect Muslim, the dutiful son. Pakistani culture visits the crimes of the child on his parents. I would shame them more than myself. It would be them, not me, at the forefront of public scorn and ridicule. The deceit ate away at me. Struggling to cope with the thoughts in my head, I clung to Islam in my search for relief.

My cousin asked me to come upstairs; he had a gift to give me in private. It was a book, *Morals for Young Shias*, which described itself as a modern-day guide for young Shia Muslims, explaining the dos and don'ts of life and love.

'It will help you out on your wedding night.' He winked before grabbing it back. 'It says here that the groom should wash his wife's feet and then pray before they get going. PRAY?! Bruv, the last thing on the groom's mind will be praying.'

I nodded and smiled in agreement. I took the book from him and flicked to the contents page, my eyes scanning frantically. There it was: 'Homosexuality & Islam: page 20'. I wanted to ask everyone to leave, explain that the party was over because I had found the answer.

'Something wrong?' he asked.

'No, no. Thank you, this is great,' I said, as evenly I could. 'Shall we go down?'

'Nah, man. At least read the bit on wanking first, it's so good ...'

The section on masturbation said you could be punished by an Islamic court. According to the book, the 'cure for masturbation' was to take up a hobby or just before bed, write a letter to distract yourself. Writing a letter seemed like a ludicrous suggestion and I couldn't think of a single hobby captivating enough to distract me from wanking.

When the last guest had left I dashed back upstairs. My parents sensed something was wrong but I didn't care because I had the answer in my hands and I couldn't wait a minute longer. I closed the door and turned to page 20. Finally alone, I shook with a nervous anticipation.

The writer acknowledged that homosexuality was not a new 'phenomenon'. This gave me a glimmer of hope. If it had been around for so long, then perhaps it wasn't unnatural? But then it went on to say that all major religions formed a united front *against* homosexual behaviour. I paused for a moment. I was too petrified to keep reading but I'd gone so far down the rabbit hole that turning back was no longer an option.

According to *Morals for Young Shias*, God turned an entire city upside down and showered its inhabitants with stones of baked clay because of their deviance. Only weeks earlier, I'd advocated such violence. My dad and I were driving through London's Finsbury Park area where we noticed more and more men wearing fewer and fewer clothes. 'I think it's a festival for … you know,' my dad said as he slowed the car to let a drag queen strut across in high heels. 'They should all be bombed!' I said. The memory brought on a pang of shame. I hated myself but it had felt good to be able to be angry at somebody else for a change, even if they were not to blame.

As my tears welled up and I considered closing the book, I told myself I needed to strengthen my willpower, to read to the end of the chapter, to force myself to stay on the path Allah had shown me. The next few pages observed that homosexuality was God's plague and must be unnatural because AIDS was easily transmitted. *God's plague.* The phrase sent a shudder through me. The author asked rhetorically whether something could be natural and yet unsafe? No, it was, according to him, a contradiction. This seemed to make sense. Was he right? It didn't happen to straight people so must it be because Allah disapproved?

Finally, under the heading 'Punishment for Homosexuality', it said that the active partner would receive 100 lashes if he was unmarried and killed if he were married. Although I wasn't sure what the difference was, it said the passive partner was to be killed no matter what his marital status.

For a moment I imagined I was the one receiving a public lashing, gasping with every strike of the whip. My mum, held back by the crowds, would be screaming for them to stop. She couldn't want that to happen to me. Could she?

I closed the book. This wasn't the Quran nor the words of the prophet. It wasn't any official text. It was just some random book, I told myself. But I was deluded. I felt sick. I'd foolishly given myself permission to dream. I had told myself my fantasies were a harmless indulgence that helped prevent me from going mad. But I had to stop these thoughts. It was unnatural. With the book clutched tightly to my chest, I imagined stones of baked clay crashing through my bedroom ceiling, solving all my problems.

14

The front of our home was on fire. Thick black smoke billowed from the upstairs window into the sun-soaked midday sky. The roof above the bay window was red, then orange then yellow. I swung open the door of my car and pressed the car horn ferociously, knowing that my mum and little Raza were somewhere inside.

Each second felt like an hour. My heartbeat echoed in my head. I ran up the driveway towards the front door and the flames. In that fleeting moment I pictured them trapped inside while I remained safe out here, unable to reach them. I imagined their screams over the cries I was already making. I imagined a life without them.

The door swung open. My mum looked confused.

'WHERE'S RAZA?!' I screamed. She stared at me, searching for the source of the fear. Then a part of the burning house dislodged itself and fell at her feet.

'MUM! WHERE'S RAZA? THE HOUSE IS ON FIRE!'

'What? He's here. He's here.' She spoke softly, still unable to comprehend what was happening. Raza was playing on the floor of the front room.

'GRAB HIM, MUM! GRAB HIM NOW AND COME OUTSIDE!' I was at the door, clutching on to them both, watching for debris as I guided them to the end of the driveway as fast as I could. Our neighbours were on the street, aghast at the sight of the blaze. I shoved my phone into someone's hand.

'Call 999!' I shouted as I ran back to the car. I saw my mum's face now covered in tears, arms wrapped round a crying Raza, as she gazed back at me, confused once more. And then I drove off.

As I had been turning into our cul-de-sac just minutes earlier, I had seen a man running away and scrambling to cover his face with the hood of his black sweatshirt.

I saw red, determined not only to find him but to do whatever it might take to stop him. I drove for a few minutes before coming to my senses. What was I doing? My mum and little brother were standing outside our burning home. They had to be my priority, not this vigilante justice.

The fire was soon extinguished by firefighters. Inside the house there was only superficial damage but the outside looked like it had been burned to within an inch of disintegration. The opposite was true of me.

I called Abbass and my dad. I started by telling them everyone was safe and then explained that the house had caught fire. They didn't need to know how on the phone. They just needed to get home.

The police arrived and confirmed that it was a petrol bombing. One officer, who didn't remove his sunglasses the whole time, said it looked like the bomber had aimed for my parents' bedroom window but missed, hitting the wall and spreading the contents of the bottle and shattered glass over the front of the house.

I told them I had seen someone running from the street.

'What ethnicity was he?'

'I didn't get a good look,' I said regretfully, 'but he was white.'

'You're sure?'

'Yes I'm sure.'

'How old was he?'

'He looked young. Teenager maybe.'

'Would you be able to describe his face or any physical features?'

'No ... it all happened too quickly and he had a hood.'

'You know how this could have happened?'

Take off your sunglasses, I thought to myself.

'No ... no, I don't.' He pulled me to the side, convinced I knew more than I was letting on.

'You in any gangs at school?' he asked.

'No,' I said.

'So you have absolutely no idea who this could be?'

'Well, my brother had some trouble with some boys up by the station but that was almost two years ago and we've never seen them again.'

'What sort of trouble?'

Take your fucking glasses off.

'The racist kind,' I said.

After the police, firefighters, family and the few sympathetic neighbours had left, I went for a walk. I needed to clear my head but I also hoped I might spot the arsonist. Returning half an hour later, I looked at the house, seeing flames that were no longer there, imagining them raging from a crucifix pitched on our front lawn.

My mum was still shaking, my dad silent. Abbass held his head in his hands and Raza had gone back to his abandoned toys on the living-room floor. Aside from some burnt window frames and a blackened front bedroom, our house was fine and so were we. But the world felt different, more threatening and inherently more dangerous. I feared the bombing was a sign that things could get much worse.

PART TWO

PART TWO

15

There are dates in people's lives that seem to act as markers on a longer journey. Points from which there is a before and an after. For me 12 October 2003, the date I started at Oxford was one such landmark. Despite passing the interview and getting the grades, I was riddled with anxiety. I was eighteen years old, legally a man, and yet the upcoming changes in my world brought an uncertainty that made me feel like I was still a child.

The night before, I slept only a little, if at all. In the morning I took my mum aside and asked her not to wear her hijab when she dropped me off. I shouldn't have asked. But where I had expected disappointment I found only support. She immediately agreed and I realized she was as anxious as I was. Their efforts to dress in smart Western clothes and the uncomfortable, self-aware way in which we carried ourselves through my new college's Gothic corridors made it feel like we were guests in the living room of nobility. As though we were requesting the benevolence of the wealthy white for the brown son.

I'd shown my parents pictures of Keble College, reminiscent of London's St Pancras Station, but resisted their requests to visit before I got my results, fearing it might jinx my chances. The photos couldn't do justice to the grandeur of the college's main square, or 'quad', but their reactions did. As we drove through the medieval-style wooden doors, my parents became awestruck children walking into a sweet shop for the first time, not knowing where to look, wanting to take in everything all at once.

'OH MY God ... Mochie!' my mum said, staring up at the stained-glass windows of the imposing Gothic chapel on the other side of the quad. The pristine lawn had a sign that read 'Do not walk' and, despite the history of the place, the smell of freshly cut grass gave it an air of newness. The bright red patterned bricks were dazzling. 'Your grandfather would have been so proud of you, he always knew you'd be a lawyer just like him,' my dad said.

My new room was dark. A single undressed bed in one corner, a desk facing onto the street and a bathroom off to one side. My mum made the bed and, while she did, I realised that this would be my job now. She would no longer be there to tidy things up and smooth out the creases. Before hugging me goodbye she placed a small pendant containing a Quranic scripture around my neck. As she fastened it, I took in her scent and tried to commit the warm feeling of her arms wrapped around me to memory.

After they left, I unpacked, placing my bilingual Quran and *Morals for Young Shias* on a shelf and Mariah Carey's entire discography on the one below. I clutched at my pendant, imagining it was my mum's hand. I paused for a while, taking in the silence, before leaving my room to find the registration desk.

That night I sat on my new bed, in my new room, thinking about my new life. The promise of Oxford all but escaped me. I couldn't relate to the enthusiasm on the fresh faces of students I had met that day. They thought eagerly of where they were going whereas all I could think of was what I had left behind. My mum had taught me to read a prayer before bed every night, to thank God for everything we'd been given. As a child I'd pray so loud that she could hear it in the next room.

Tonight, I recited the familiar verses once more, hoping she might be able to hear me, despite the miles between us.

By the end of freshers' week, people referred to me not by my name but by the nickname 'Mos'. I'm not sure where it came from. I didn't particularly like it but, even if I'd had the confidence, English etiquette might be offended if I corrected someone within minutes of meeting them. I was a brown face in a sea of white; I didn't want to cause a fuss. After a number of conversations in which I patiently repeated my name, then spelled it out, then explained that *yes, the 'h' did go before the 's'* and *no, my parents hadn't made a mistake on my birth certificate*, I grew tired of constantly correcting people. I embraced my abbreviated name after Nick, the friend I'd made during the first weeks of term and a fellow lawyer, called me 'Martin'.

'Nick, my name isn't Martin. Did you think it was Martin all this time?' I tried to disguise the whine of disappointment in my voice.

'I'm sorry, mate,' he said. 'I've just ... well, I've never really been friends with a foreigner before.' It was intriguing that he could get into one of the world's best academic institutions but know so little about the world itself. I felt like a foreigner long before being called one. I phoned my parents that night and told them I wanted to come home. I suggested a London university instead.

'You tell that boy if he tries to leave Oxford, I'll slap him sideways,' my dad said in the background.

About twenty of us, boys with whom I would spend the next few years, headed towards a table covered with a white disposable tablecloth, reminding me of the Pakistani weddings I'd attended at Walthamstow town hall. My first time in a proper curry house. As I took a seat, it occurred to me that I'd never eaten curry with a knife and fork before and a mild panic set in. I couldn't eat with my hands, not in front of these people. I looked at the boys to my left and my right and across the table from me. It was difficult to hold on to who was who because the group liked to interchange first names with surnames too regularly to keep up.

It was a BYOB restaurant, which one of them had told me meant *bring your own booze*, making it a favourite with students. There were so many cans of beer on the table I wondered where the food would go. The potent fumes of alcohol were inescapable.

Introducing ourselves to each other, straight away I managed to embarrass myself. First by asking one what he meant when he asked what subject I was *reading*, and then by asking another what classics meant. 'It's primarily the study of ancient Greek and Latin,' he told me in his cut-glass British accent. I wondered why he was studying a language nobody spoke any more.

'CHUG! CHUG! CHUG! CHUG!' the boys chanted. It was my turn to prove I was one of them. My eyes were fixed on the bubbles gently rising in the beer that had been slammed in front of me. I wondered what to do. The lighting in the restaurant was a dark blue neon; at that moment it felt like a spotlight. Next to the beer was a bowl of what was supposed to be chicken curry. It was a lurid orange. It smelled unfamiliar and unpleasant. The crockery was mismatched, more authentically Pakistani than the food on offer. I'd chosen the chicken korma because it was one of the only things on the menu I recognised. When asked for recommendations by some of my new peers, I confidently suggested they order the same. They seemed disappointed, expecting that I would know of some secret dish that wasn't listed.

Just before the chanting started, a guy across from me had thrown a penny into the beer. 'Save the queen, matey, before she drowns,' he said.

I wanted them to like me but no part of me wanted to drink the beer to make that happen. This was the first time people assumed I drank rather than the opposite. I guess I'd have to come out sooner than I thought.

'Mos, it's your turn, mate, you've been pennied,' another guy chimed in.

'He doesn't drink, man, move on.' I turned to see Nick shouting from one end of the table.

'Yaaaaah ... well, no one's perfect, mate, ha ha. Hitler was teetotal too, you know!' said someone, much to the amusement of the others.

'Wait, seriously, you don't drink?' asked the penny guy.

'No,' I replied meekly.

Although the group had moved on, he wasn't able to let it go so easily. He looked startled, as if my decision not to drink was inspired by *Mein Kampf* itself.

'You don't drink at all?'

'No,'

'Why the bloooooody hell not?'

'I'm Muslim.' I felt uncomfortable having to declare it. The others were pretending not to listen.

'That isn't a *reason* why not. What is the intellectual *reasoning* behind this rather alaaarming resolve?' He, along with most of the others, spoke as if to do so was a tiresome chore, dragging out words in a monotonous tone of indifference. At my old comprehensive school I wondered why they didn't just speak normally. Now I did the same, although here my accent allowed me to blend in more easily.

The leader of the pack, a rugby-playing six-foot-two blond guy called Henry, thrust a jug of water at me and led the cheer. I glimpsed the fine hairs on his thick arm.

'Dooooown it! Doooooown it! Dooooown it!' he and the others sang.

It was a kindness of sorts. An attempt at making me feel included. But I didn't drink and sitting with them chanting as I guzzled a jug of water wasn't going to change that.

'Guys, just leave it,' Nick interjected once more, much to my relief.

Later in the meal, the penny guy told me that God was a fiction designed to control the masses and that the whole concept was implausible. He expected to upset me. I wasn't sure I'd ever knowingly spoken to someone who didn't believe in God. I was more excited than offended because, finally, I was having a conversation with someone who wanted to offer me their opinion and then listen to mine rather than punch me. I didn't doubt God existed, just whether he would help me, but I wasn't about to share that. I was there to make friends, not to find converts. Oxford allowed me to pretend to be someone else. My peers knew I didn't drink but they knew nothing else about me and I took steps to keep it that way.

'Mos, Mos, come over here, you can settle this for us.' Rugby Henry stood near the entrance to Keble's 1970s onsite bar, known as 'the Spaceship'. He was locked in debate with Oliver, whose rosy red cheeks and stringy blond hair gave him an angelic finish.

Henry wore fake gold chains around his neck, decorating an oversized black Wu-Tang Clan hoodie, while Oliver wore a red Yankees cap backwards, white vest and baggy jeans. The theme for the evening was 'Slappers and Rappers'.

'Why aren't you dressed up?' Henry enquired in an accent that contrasted violently with his current aesthetic.

'I didn't really have anything to wear and, I dunno, it just seemed a bit weird.'

'Want one of my chains?'

'Oh ... no. That's OK, but thanks.'

'Anyway, Mos, listen, which one do you think is better, Eton or Harrow?' Henry asked.

'What?' I hadn't heard those words before and thought they might be Oxford slang to add to my repertoire.

'Well, you see, Oli went to Harrow and has this preposterous notion that it's better than Eton and we were hoping you could settle it for us. Obviously Eton is far superior, I mean Prince Harry was in my year for Christ's sake, surely there is no debate. Don't you agree?' he said.

'Oh, are they your schools?'

Oliver looked at me blankly. Henry brought his brows together into a frown.

'You've ... you've never heard of Harrow? Or Eton?' His bewildered tone matched my own feelings then.

'Well, I went to Walthamstow Secondary School – have either of you heard of that?'

They looked at each other, returned their gaze to me and Oliver shook his head. Henry's face froze, as if the wind had changed.

'Then why would I have heard of your schools?' I asked, baffled by their puzzlement.

'They are only the top two public schools in the ...' he trailed off incredulous.

'Well, yes, it's a fair point,' Oliver replied. I scrambled to fill the uncomfortable silence.

'By the way, do you guys know when our student loan gets paid? I'll be on the Pot Noodle diet soon,' I said, trying to lighten the mood.

'Oh, I don't know, I don't have a student loan,' Oliver said before turning to Henry.

'Oh no, me neither, I'm afraid, matey.' Henry shrugged.

'You don't? How do you pay for things?'

'Parents,' they replied.

'So your parents have thousands of pounds they can just give you when you need it?' Their reactions told me that talking about money was somehow improper, but it was too late.

'Yes,' said Henry.

As the crowd swelled, I noticed Riz, the Pakistani guy from Walthamstow, at the bar, the one I'd copied in applying to Keble. Although I barely knew him, he was from home and right now he felt like family.

'Why aren't you dressed up?' I asked.

'HA! Good one. What is it with posh people's obsession with dressing up? And then they go and choose a theme designed to mock poor blacks?' He was observational rather than offended.

'Oh. I hadn't really thought about it.' Clothing was a minefield. Seemingly, the Oxford aesthetic was to look as much like your parents as possible. Buttoned shirts and loafers. At a freshers' party I was asked more than once whether I had any drugs to sell. I stood out. A hoody or jogging bottoms made them look sporty and me look threatening. I had to start blending in so I bought a couple of polo shirts, but then overheard someone say that wearing your collar down was for poor people. Should I wear mine up, I wondered, because everyone else did, or wear it down, so that I didn't look like I was trying to be something I wasn't?

'I hear you're a bit of a hit with the second years ... there are definitely a couple of girls who have asked me if you're single.' Riz was teasing me.

'I'm not really looking,' I said.

'Good Muslim boy, aren't you, Mohsin?' He smiled at me, pride in his voice.

'Yeah, well, I have to marry a Muslim,' I said.

'Check out Uni Isoc and Paksoc, you'll find plenty there,' he said.

'There's an Islamic society?'

'Yeah, of course. They host *iftars* during Ramadan – food is delicious. You should check it out.'

The air in the library was dense with the smell of old books, the atmosphere grave and serious. 'Is it the job of a judge to represent or to reflect society?' was the essay question I had to answer this week. The accompanying reading list included roman numerals, which I could not read because I had never been taught how. Instead, I searched the law section hoping the titles would jump out at me. As I read title after title along the shelves I couldn't help but feel like I wouldn't be able to understand the books I was meant to read, even if I could locate them. Eventually, I gave up.

The sun was setting as I returned to my room. Laughter echoed through the hallway. The door facing mine was ajar. Paul was a first-year archaeology and anthropology student with a strong Birmingham accent, permanent grin and mild manner that made him instantly likable.

'Hi,' came a friendly voice as I peered in. She had a big smile, light brown skin and kindness in her eyes.

'Hi,' I replied.

'I'm Layla.'

Paul jumped up from the floor, where a loose circle of people sat around with half-filled glasses and an open bottle of alcohol.

'Mos, we're probably gonna go down to Cowley if you fancy joining us? No need to drink of course.' Growing up in Birmingham, most of Paul's friends had been Pakistani. This fact put me at ease when we met.

'We might try and find the black boy,' suggested a voice.

'Good luck finding a black boy in Oxford!' Layla responded and they laughed.

I stared at her, wondering what the joke was.

'Oh my God, it's a pub! And I'm taking the piss. Did you not read that article?' she said.

'No.'

'Basically this article in the student paper said that in our year across the uni there are only thirty-three black undergrads – can you believe it?'

I shook my head. They debated the merits and pitfalls of the admissions process before Layla, seemingly no longer interested in debate, suddenly whispered 'Watch this. Paul thinks he can say hello in the accent of any country on the planet.'

'Really?'

'Yes! And we can't figure out whether he genuinely believes it or not. Watch. Paul, what about hello in Egyptian?'

'Hello,' he said in the same Midland accent but with a hint of throaty Arab sounds thrown in. I wasn't sure whether to laugh.

'It's OK, I'm Egyptian, but in any event we aren't very PC in here so if your sensibilities are easily offended turn away now.'

'What about Pakistan?' I asked.

'Hello,' he said in a Brummie accent but with a shake of the head.

'Try South Africa,' suggested a blonde girl.

'That's Sophie,' Layla said as the girl waved in my direction. 'People think she's nice but actually she's just Aryan.' They all fell about laughing and Sophie mouthed 'it's true' in my direction. There was a formality in the Oxford air that hadn't found its way into this room. The glances felt more sincere, the questions less heavy. I perched on Paul's desk.

'Listen, guys,' Sophie interjected. 'What about the Jamaica bar? I hear they charge you based on how you look. Isn't that great? All the toffs get charged loads. We'll be fine ...' It had been at least five minutes and not one mention of schools, A-level results or parental occupations.

'You should join us,' Layla suggested.

'Yes you should,' Sophie said.

'I'd love to,' I said. 'Wait, why would a bar charge you based on how you look?' I directed the question at the room.

'Oh dear, oh dear, oh dear,' Layla replied. 'You have much to learn, my friend.'

16

A few weeks into my first term I already felt like I was getting an education in things other than law. If the university was an old, public-school-educated white man, with thick grey hair and weathered skin, his children were the thirty-eight Oxford colleges. Much like children they each had their own style, personalities and sense of themselves; diverse in character if not in their intimidating whiteness. Christ Church, founded by Henry VIII, was successful and arrogant, more so after *Harry Potter* began filming there. Oriel was the youthful Tory. Keble was the sporty one. But, founded to broaden access, it made room for diversity. These stereotypes didn't just exist in the buildings. I encountered them in Oxford's libraries, its pubs and student societies. A common bonding strategy was to ask a new person what school they had gone to. The answers were repetitive: St Paul's, Winchester, Marlborough, City of London, Rugby (like the game), Dulwich, Westminster. At first I couldn't understand why, but I was learning.

'I'm Ish, you're Mos, right?' she said. Her accent told me she was from Manchester. Her silky black hair, so long it had clearly never been cut, told me she was a Sikh.

'Yes, nice to meet you,' I replied. We sat next to each other in the grandeur of Keble Hall, draped in black 'commoners' gowns that squared at the shoulders and fell just below the waist, a mandatory clothing requirement for formal dining. Eating together was an important part of college life. Keble was one of the few colleges that retained formal dining six nights out of seven. The dining room was vast: three hundred metres long, its thirty-metre-high ceiling supported by a series of grand wooden arches under which sat three long tables. They ran vertically from the entrance to the top table, placed horizontally at the far end. The glow from the lamps on the tables illuminated the college-embossed plates and double-set silverware that I knew from the *Titanic* film you used from the outside in.

'So are you Pakistani?'

I nodded. The way she said *Pakistani* reminded me of the northern twang from the characters in *East is East*.

'My parents are Indian – don't worry, we can still be friends though.' She gave me a nudge. 'But we can't get married or anything like that. I can't date Muslims, so don't get any ideas.' She was smiling. I made an effort to smile back but was feeling low. The novelty of university was wearing off, and the reality of my predicament setting in.

After a thud of the gavel, prayer began in Latin and everyone jumped to their feet.

'Are you OK?' Ish whispered. I paused, letting her think it was out of respect for the grace.

'Yes, yes, I'm fine.'

'You don't seem fine,' she said as we sat down. Her gentle directness touched me.

'I guess I'm a bit down, but I don't really know why.'

'Maybe I can help you. Is it your work?'

'No,' I said.

'Problems with friends?'

'Mmm ... no.'

'Family?'

'No, no, it's not that either.' I was pretending to consider each in turn with her.

'Well then, it must be your love life.'

'Ha ha. No, no, it's not that either,' I said nervously.

'What then?' She looked confused and placed an arm on my shoulder.

I wasn't ready to explain it to myself so how could I verbalise it to her?

'Did I hear you're from Pakistan?' asked a guy from across the table, leaning into the glow of lamplight to reveal floppy brown hair and a scarf hanging loosely around his neck.

'Well ... yes, my parents are.'

'OH! I simply love Pakistan!' he said. Ish had turned to speak to the person on her other side.

'You've been?!'

'I schooled with the Zahar family. Do you know them?'

'No.' I laughed, wondering why he would ask that when it was a country of almost 200 million people and I wasn't actually from there.

'Great horse riding. Such a silly place really.'

'What?'

'Such a silly country, so much fun.'

I didn't know what to say. The waiter placed a plate in front of me. It was a boiled egg, nested in mashed potato with some leaves I couldn't name on the side.

'That looks lovely!' Ish observed, sitting in front of a succulent chicken breast dripping with a brown sauce. College didn't offer halal meat so through no choice of my own I had the vegetarian option. My egg-potato combination didn't so much taste disgusting as taste of nothing. These dishes were invariably the opposite of the spice-coated meat dishes I'd been raised on. I went to Formal Hall to make friends, not for the food, and often supplemented my compulsory vegetarian meal with a visit to one of Oxford's halal kebab vans.

'Excuse me.' I caught the eye of one of the young guys serving the food. 'Is there any chance I could get something a bit more … spicy?' I said, almost whispering. I actually didn't mean spicy, I meant something that had more flavour but saying so felt rude.

'Erm … sorry?'

I imagined Abbass standing in his place, being ordered around by an entitled Oxford student.

'Actually, don't worry. It's fine, sorry. Ignore me.' I was instantly apologetic. Being waited on felt to me like an unearned privilege. I felt like I should be doing the waiting.

'Is everything OK?' Shane, one of the more senior staff members, asked. He was a short, balding man with dark eyes.

'Yes! It's fine. Thank you,' I said in a rush.

'Are you sure? I really don't mind.' His eyes lingered over me, as though he knew something about me. I felt uneasy.

'Yes, I'm sure,' I said, turning away abruptly, a sick feeling in my stomach.

After dinner I went back to my room to pray for the fifth and final time that day. I stayed with my forehead pressed to the floor and tried not to think about the hall manager's gaze. Ish's simple questions had so easily identified the problem, even if I hadn't given her the answers. My sadness came from a lack of any interest in my work, from the absence of a love life and what such a love life would do to my family. It was about the necessary distance I placed between me and anybody who might become a friend. Not even praying offered any respite. I raised my head, but stayed seated on my prayer mat. God wasn't listening to me. I might never be cured.

Layla and I had quickly become close. Around her I felt a peacefulness that prayer seldom brought me these days. A sense that everything might be OK after all. She intrigued me; she seemed so comfortable in her brown skin in this most English of institutions. I, apparently, intrigued her too. She didn't understand how someone our age could have gone eighteen years without knowing who Radiohead were or that butternut squash was a vegetable.

'What did they say exactly?' Layla asked. She was on my bed, while I slouched in the swivel chair by my desk.

'Mum just mentioned that my uncle's daughter Mariam is a lovely girl and asked whether I'd be interested.' I sighed.

'Are you?'

'I'm not sure, I don't think so.' I imagined waking up one morning and fancying women instead of men. If this happened, my life could start.

'Would they want you to get married soon?' Layla was concerned for me. Her family was from Egypt, and although they were Christian not Muslim, her Arab background meant that there was no need for me to translate the dynamic with my parents into a language she might understand.

'No, I don't think so. I think Mum just wants to know whether they should make the approach now so that she isn't snapped up by someone else.' It wasn't the first time there'd been talk of marriage. I was the eldest son so it was as natural to see my wedding on the horizon as it was for the sun to rise. Studying law at Oxford had sparked a flurry of interest in my suitability. If there were Muslim marriage Top Trumps, an Oxford lawyer would be a winning card.

'They won't try and force you, will they?'

'No. They aren't insane, just religious.'

'I know, but I had to ask, I'd feel bad if I didn't at least check.'

'Don't worry, I'm not going to be kidnapped and rushed off to Pakistan any time soon, but it does happen. A lot.'

'Those poor girls,' she said.

'Happens to boys too, but less, I guess,' I said, massaging the direction of the conversation.

'Boys too?'

'Yeah … usually they're gay and their parents think the solution is to force them into marriage.'

'That's so terrible, and once again, those poor women.'

'What?'

'The women. As if they deserve to be put in a marriage with a man who's been forced into it.' Her insight astonished me. I would be different though. I wouldn't force a woman into marriage, it had to be her choice. I would treat her properly and she would never know.

It was the desire to find such a woman that sealed my presence at the Pakistani Society event – that and the fact that Imran Khan was speaking at Keble. The room murmured in anticipation of his arrival.

'I've been asked what I think of 9/11 on several occasions,' a young man in the front row said to his companion.

'Me too … but only the once,' I interrupted in the hope of joining their discussion.

'For now,' the friend said, the pair turning to include me. They were caricatures of the English upper classes. They were as stiff as their starched blazers with accents that made the Queen sound like she might be from Walthamstow.

'Of course these Muslims don't help with their constant conspiracy theories and misgivings about the Iraq invasion.'

'Aren't you both Muslim?' I asked.

'Well, yes, I suppose we are, but you know what I mean, the ones who actually pray and such.' The room was filled with a collection of people who appeared to be even wealthier than the average Oxford student. All of them from boarding school and talking about Pakistan as if it were a naughty child that needed to learn to behave. The mention of a hangover alarmed me.

'You drink?' I asked with more than a hint of disdain.

'You don't ... ?' His reply was delivered with one-upmanship.

'Do your parents know?'

'Ha! My dad is the biggest drinker I know,' he said with inexplicable pride. Pakistanis that drink? Not just young Pakistanis but Pakistani mums and dads. Was this what education did to brown people?

Imran Khan was taller than I expected and more handsome in real life than in the pictures and videos I'd grown up with. He was the only permissible crush for Pakistani wives because their husbands felt the same.

'This room, each of you, is Pakistan's future. When you are heads of government departments or heads of multinational corporations you need to remember your country.' He was surer of our remarkably successful futures than of our commitment to Pakistan. The suggestion that we were the leaders of tomorrow didn't make anyone flinch. Their eyes were like sponges that soaked up his assumption of brilliance. As Ramadan crept closer, I hoped that the Islamic Society would prove a more fruitful place to make friends than this brown ivory tower.

Ramadan was the month in which the Quran was revealed to the Prophet Muhammad. Fasting during the daylight hours of this holiest of months was one of the Five Pillars of Islam but it extended beyond food and water. Intimate touching during a fast was forbidden. Muslims were to refrain from all sinful behaviour, including sinful thoughts. Giving up food was easy. Giving up the lustful thoughts inside my head was not. I counted them up one by one: the Portuguese guy in the year above I glimpsed in the library; the law student in my lectures; and many others. I forced them into a windowless corner of my mind and shut the door. On the prayer mat, I asked Allah to curse me, to make me as unattractive as possible so that even if I desired him no man would ever feel the same about me.

At the Islamic Society event we sat on the floor of a tiled basement room to eat food donated by a Muslim business in Cowley, the ethnic quarter of Oxford.

'I got my lota from Cowley, you know,' said one guy, as he scooped up some mince with a piece of naan bread. We used lotas, or water pots, in the absence of bidets in the toilet.

'Brother, why didn't you just bring one from home? What did you do until you discovered Cowley?' said another, insinuating that he must have failed to wash his bum for a while. There was something liberating in being able to speak so freely about the lack of appropriate washing facilities and what to do about it.

'I used an empty bottle but the bloody college cleaner kept throwing it away. In the end I had to put a Post-it note on it saying "Please do not remove, used for shitting". She stopped touching it after that.' Following the meal, a bearded guy who I hadn't noticed earlier introduced himself and asked if he could offer me a piece of advice.

'Brother, you shouldn't be shaving. Our prophet kept a beard and it is incumbent upon us to follow his example.'

'Thank you for the advice, brother. I will think about it,' I said.

'What is there to think about?'

The seconds passed as I tried to think of something to say other than 'mind your own business'.

'We must be careful in this place,' he continued. 'We are surrounded by non-believers, by kafir, and there is temptation everywhere we turn. We must take active steps to remain close to Allah.'

His tone agitated me. He had no idea of the steps I was taking, probably bigger than he could possibly imagine.

'I heard you mention you went to that curry house, Jamal's. Were you drinking?'

'No! I went for a dinner with some of the guys from my year.'

'Were they drinking?'

'Of course, this is England. We aren't in Saudi Arabia.'

'Even more reason to be on your guard,' he said.

Returning to college, I saw the chapel glowing in the moonlight. I wondered what it would look like with a large golden dome at its centre, topped by a crescent and star, in the Oxford skyline. Life would be so much easier if it did. Paksoc proved to be for the wealthy and Isoc for the religious so I decided to throw myself into college life.

Despite growing up in one of the biggest cities on the planet, sometimes I felt like I'd been raised in a remote Pakistani village. Although I was brimming with internal conflict, the version of myself I presented to the outside world was different. At Oxford I was bowled over by new ideas and experiences, a glutton with too much food. I seemed like a gregarious and intellectually curious young man, hungry to see what this unfamiliar environment could offer. I quickly acclimatised, sitting at the centre of dinner tables and dancing in the middle of circles. Music in particular was my salvation, a place to which I could retreat when I felt alone or confused. According to some strict observers, music was forbidden in Islam but I figured that on the scale of sinful behaviour, the Spice Girls were nowhere near as bad as gay sex. My overenthusiasm saw me run for the university debating society, and although I was successful at being elected to the committee, it was a mistake. The Oxford Union was uniformly public-school kids playing politics. A training ground before the stakes had national implications.

Layla and I said goodbye at the end of first term. I'd never met anyone like her before. We weren't from similar places but we thought about the world in the same way and we were both secretly hopeless romantics. After watching *The Eternal Sunshine of the Spotless Mind*, a film about a woman who had erased all memories of a soured love rather than live with them, we debated for hours whether we too would erase a bad relationship from our minds. I knew what it was to carry thoughts around which felt like ulcers under the eyelid. I was adamant that I would choose to erase the painful memories. By the end of our conversation, Layla had convinced me that the beauty of life was not just in the wonderful moments but in the terrible ones too. That without them there was no point to any of it. I could sense that Layla had feelings for me. I wanted to feel the same way and I told myself that I did. I tried to ignore the cravings of my body in favour of the softer, more amenable desires of my heart. I knew I cared for her and hoped it could become a love that could last a lifetime. But I also knew that I was trying to make it something it was not, just as my culture was asking the same of me. If only I could erase the gay, maybe I could live in eternal sunshine too.

I returned home at Christmas and adjusted to a new role: the triumphant eldest son, full of promise. My mum made my favourites, chicken curry and spinach with lamb. Her cooking was as comforting as a child's teddy and as vital to our bond as the blood we shared.

I overheard bursts of laughter downstairs and joined Mum and Abbass in front of the TV. Leaving home made Abbass and me close again. The frequent arguments between us had fallen into the canyon of our teenage years. They were watching a camp US sitcom called *Will & Grace* which Mum said was really funny. Flamboyant men seemed to tickle my mum's sense of humour, Graham Norton being her favourite. The TV show was about a gay lawyer. I looked at my mum and then Abbass and then Mum again, wondering what it might be like to come out to them in the lightness of this moment.

Between prayers, I secretly researched cures for homosexuality. Physical problems almost always had a cure. Online testimonials told stories of lives saved. One described the new life of a guy from Birmingham called Yassar. Yassar spoke of his desperation upon realising he had sexual feelings for men until he was able to get help. Now, according to this website, Yassar was married with kids, leading a normal, happy life. I wanted to be Yassar. But an instinct as raw as survival told me something wasn't quite right: Yassar was lying to himself. I would have undergone electric shock therapy if I thought it had any chance of working, but I was beginning to suspect that I might never be straight.

Later the same evening, the news reported on a historic bill that would be going through Parliament: The Civil Partnership Act. We were joined now on the other sofa by my dad with Raza in his lap. The newsreader explained that the Act promised equal rights for same-sex couples, but not marriage. I had no plans to take advantage of a civil partnership but something seemed wrong about making a law for a specific group of people just to deprive them of marriage. Equal but separate.

'What the hell is that? Why are they giving them marriage? How can they legitimise those people?' Abbass said with indignation. His words gave me the feeling of being watched. I shifted in my seat.

'Not marriage. That would be wrong. They are giving them this other thing so they have rights,' Mum corrected him in a tone that suggested she understood why same-sex couples needed legal recognition. I closed my eyes and took a deep breath.

'It's basically marriage and it won't be long before they're calling it marriage,' he insisted, shaking his head ruefully.

'What's wrong with you?' I said.

'What?' Abbass looked at me.

'What is it to you? They're human beings and they deserve equal rights under the law.' I intentionally framed it as a legal debate rather than a moral one.

'It's wrong!' he said with a firmness that matched the look in his eye.

'Then don't do it! No one's telling you to enter a civil partnership.' My tone was mocking, as if he was barely worth debating with. My parents, uncharacteristically, hadn't joined in. They could see that in the eight weeks I'd been away, I'd found my voice.

'What, so you think it's OK all of a sudden, Oxford boy? It's un-Islamic, they're going to hell. What's more important to you, the law or Islam?' He had backed me into a corner, knowing that my parents were eagerly awaiting the answer.

'I just think they should be treated equally, that's all.'

'Yeah, actually you're right, they should be treated equally.'

That took me completely by surprise. It wasn't like Abbass to accept he was wrong in the heat of the moment.

'They should all be shot,' he said, before leaving the room.

17

Back at university, the January chill made eating in the college hall feel like we were dining outside. I sat next to some people I knew and others I did not. A guy in my year was talking about how good he was at cooking. Like many of the students I encountered here, he spoke with the confidence of someone much older. 'I make a mean curry, bloody spicy too. Learned in my gap year in India.'

'The only reason he took a gap year was because Oxford rejected him the first time round,' a girl next to me whispered. 'Two bites of the cherry, all right for some,' she added. Pulling up the gown that perpetually slipped off my shoulders, I wondered how life afforded some people the luxury of stepping off the treadmill for a year and then effortlessly climbing back on when it suited them.

As on so many other nights, I silently fumed at the prospect of the flavourless veggie dish. I overheard the serving staff say that the evening's meat option was salmon, so I asked for that instead. What they placed in front of me didn't look like salmon, though it certainly wasn't chicken or beef. Too self-conscious to ask, I took a bite. And then a second.

'This doesn't taste like salmon,' I whispered, hoping the person next to me would confirm that it was.

'SALMON?!' the gap-year boy shouted across the table. 'It's GA-MMON, not salmon!' His amusement attracted the attention of others around the table. I stared blankly back at him. 'You're Muslim, right? That's bloody pork!' he said through fits of laughter, pointing at the dish.

'Do shut up. It's not funny,' another voice said.

I was turning red and I wasn't sure if it was from fury or embarrassment. I pushed the plate away and quietly picked at the replacement vegetarian meal that was given to me. I didn't want to make a scene. As soon as we finished I got up and rushed to the sink in my room and shoved two fingers as far down my throat as they would go before I was staring at the meal I had just eaten.

Although I was sure there was no food left in my system, I felt dirty. I didn't know whether to tell my parents. Instead, I sought Allah's forgiveness. Sitting on the prayer mat I became enraged. Before I knew it, I had sent an angry email ranting about the inequity of making me pay for vegetarian food that I did not want. Either stop charging for them or start providing halal meals. The college did eventually offer halal food and this small victory gave me the profile of a champion for the rights of minorities. I was a good Muslim.

R. v *Brown* was a case on my criminal law reading list. The case was about a group of gay men who'd filmed themselves having sex. Not just sex, but violent sexual acts including nailing their foreskins to a wooden board for sexual pleasure. I felt a mixture of fear, that all gay sex was as colourful as this, and relief, because I would never know anyway. In the tutorial though, I found myself defending these men. The question was whether they should be prosecuted for crimes of assault committed against each other, despite the fact that they were consenting adults. My tutorial partner seemed disapproving of the behaviour which ignited a sense of justice in me.

'Why should they go to jail? They haven't done anything wrong. Who are we to sit here and judge their behaviour?' The words streamed from a place inside me I had no idea existed. This education, it seemed, was helping me discover that I had strong opinions of my own. It also made me question whether the opinions I formulated in defence of others had any relevance to my own life.

Sadomasochism aside, I found myself studying less and socialising more. When one friend went into hibernation to meet an essay deadline, another emerged from a caffeine-fuelled all-nighter with dazed eyes and a thirst for alcohol. Meanwhile, I took a genuine interest in others. Much like books, reading a person could be just as captivating, and also educational. Asking questions about others had a secondary benefit too: it deflected attention from me.

Socialising taught me how to navigate this world of privilege and doors continued to open, although I didn't always know what I was meant to do when I stepped inside. I was elected college undergraduate president. I didn't run because of ambition. For me it was validation, acceptance. But I was building a prison out of my success; the more I achieved, the more my parents' eyes shone with pride for their boy – how could I tarnish this gleaming image?

Doing the work required of me for the law degree meant spending time alone with my books, and also my thoughts. It was as if there were a constant ringing in my ears, the volume going up depending on how quiet it was or how lonely I felt. The company of others acted as white noise, dialling it down. To maximise time with friends I skipped much of the required reading and wrote essays at the eleventh hour. The tutorial system, with two students to one academic in a class, played to my strengths. I was able to articulate coherent opinions on legal principles in cases I hadn't taken the time to read properly. I seemed to be able to convince my teachers I knew what I was doing, even though I had little clue, giving me the power to coast through much of the first year of my degree. Or so I thought.

'Did you revise for these mocks, Mohsin?' my tutor asked in a tone that gave nothing away about how he felt. In the run-up to 'collections', the Oxford term for mock exams, there was a casualness among my fellow lawyers that rubbed off on me. They told me they didn't do much work. It was the language of British understatedness, a dialect I did not speak, although I was learning. It wasn't lying, its texture was less coarse. It was a softer downplaying that came with the benefit of not showing one's hand too early.

'Well … erm … not much, I guess,' I said.

'You've been so focused on student politics and socialising that you've forgotten why you're here.' A pause while he waited for me to say something. 'You do know why you are here, don't you?'

'Yes,' I said.

'Well, unfortunately you might not be here much longer. To go to Holland in your third year you have to get a 2:1, at least 60 per cent. You failed two of the mock exams and barely scraped a pass on the third. With these marks you can forget about going to Holland. You need to focus on passing first-year exams so that you can stay at this institution.' His use of the word institution made me feel like I was on the outside again. I walked out of his office, collected my things and went to the library. I stared at books, reading about criminal cases involving untimely, horrific murders, and daydreamed about being one of the victims, just to get out of having to do my exams. My chest was heavy, a weight that didn't shift in the days that followed. I barely slept, instead imagining the same scene playing out: my tutor calling my house in the holidays to inform me I had failed and could not return to the world's most exceptional university, to the single greatest opportunity life had given me, followed by a supplementary scene, where I get to tell my parents and then absorb their devastation.

With only a couple of weeks to go and an entire syllabus to consume, I threw myself into constitutional and criminal law. If I was going to go down, it would not be without a fight.

The only thing worse than having to sit these exams was having to do them in something resembling a tuxedo. The white bow tie felt unbearably tight around my neck as I took the long walk from Keble to the examination hall on the high street for my criminal law exam. My gown whirled around me. I hadn't slept the night before and had been physically sick twice that morning. I'd scribbled a page of notes on the key cases but I knew none of it off by heart. On impulse, I'd stuffed the notes in my trouser pocket before leaving. I couldn't risk being kicked out. Maybe I could go to the toilet and sneak a look if I really needed to. It wasn't my final exams, just first year, I reasoned. My suit itched and the black shoes were still rigid with newness. We weren't allowed pencil cases so I carried stationery in the graduation cap I had to bring with me, but was forbidden from wearing until I graduated. As I sat at my desk in the middle of one of a hundred rows, I had damp patches under my arms and beads of sweat rolled down my face. I looked around at the portraits of successful old, white men in ostentatious gold frames. None of them were smiling.

'A few house rules, students. If you have any material on your person that could be used to assist you in answering your questions you must forfeit it at this point. If it is found after the examination has commenced you will be deemed to have used it and may be ejected from this exam hall and this institution.' The notes tucked in my pocket felt like a giant zit on the tip of my nose. My palms were sweaty. My right knee bounced up and down involuntarily. I looked at the exits, imagined myself making a run for it. The examiner continued to intone the house rules but his words were drowned out by the beat of my heart. I whispered 'Bismillah' to myself, the prayer Muslims recite before they do anything significant. I paused for a moment and then removed the notes from my pocket and waved them in the air to the examiner who walked over and took them from me.

That summer, once exams were over, I got a job selling women's perfume in the foyer of another big department store on Oxford Street. Standing on the shop floor I thought constantly about the moment I would have to break it to my parents that I'd been kicked out.

'Hey, Mos,' came the voice of a girl, two years above me. She was with her mother. They wore matching Barbour gilets.

'Oh, hi.' I'd forgotten her name and also that I might conceivably bump into someone from university here. As I stood holding the blue star-shaped bottle of perfume in one hand, and white tester strips in the other, I was overcome with embarrassment.

'What are you doing here?' she asked.

'What do you think he's doing here?' her mother said before I could reply. I wanted to spray them away with perfume. Before arriving at Oxford I had thought nothing of serving people in a shop. Now I knew not only what a social hierarchy was but also my place within it.

'Any news on exam results?' Rumours of next year's college president being kicked out had been circulating. I shook my head and smiled.

'I'm sure you'll be fine,' she said. As I stared at the back of their heads venturing deeper into the store, I said a prayer to myself, pleading with Allah to let me pass. I didn't want to spend my life bumping into people I'd once gone to Oxford with, before they walked away and gossiped about how I'd been kicked out, all the while making observations about how much promise I'd shown and what had become of me now. When I finished work, I wandered into Soho. I didn't want to go home. Walking down a strip of bars I kept my head down, peering up occasionally at rainbow flags bouncing in the wind. A sign above one bar read 'G-A-Y' and a group of guys about my age spotted me staring at it. One waved, and without returning the gesture, I hurried home.

I'd taken the day off because I knew the call was coming. I paced up and down my room and up and down the stairs and up and down the garden. I played football with Raza and was pleased that, at six years old, he was too young to appreciate what it meant to be kicked out of Oxford University. I couldn't face being a disappointment to him too.

'Mochie, it's for you,' my mum shouted from the hallway.

'Right, Mohsin, so your results are not clear cut,' my tutor said. I wanted the floor to swallow me up. I had spent the last year praying for God to take Oxford away from me. And now it might actually be happening.

'Now, I told you that you needed to average 60 per cent to go to Holland, yes?'

'Yes,' I said with a quiver in my voice.

'Well, you averaged 59.67 per cent, but luckily for you, the law faculty rounds up, so congratulations. You got a 2:1 and are still on the four-year course.'

I screamed, and my mum and Raza, able to tell it was good news, jumped up and down and screamed too.

'I'm not quite sure how you managed it, Mohsin, but I'm pleased you did. Needless to say, you will not be wanting to cut it that close for finals. Understood?'

'Understood,' I said through a deep sigh. I'd made it by the skin of my teeth. I was relieved. Ecstatic even. It was only when the opportunity of a lifetime was slipping through my fingers that I realised how much I wanted it and how foolish I had been to pray it away.

18

House music blasted from the straw hut across a Thai beach filled with dancers visible in the light of the half-moon. The moist air clung to my skin. This was my first time abroad without my family. I was here with Clare, a university friend from Somerset. She had a fun-loving, independent soul and striking green eyes. We had bonded over our mutual disdain for the obnoxiously loud men's drinking society at college.

'I'd love to go on a trip like that,' I had said when she described her plans for the summer.

'Then come!'

'I can't – my parents won't let me.'

'You're nineteen. Just ignore them!'

'Ha! You clearly weren't raised Pakistani.' I didn't understand how English kids could be so dismissive of the wishes of the parents who bankrolled their lives, although I knew this wasn't the case for Clare.

'I think it's about time you lived your own life, don't you?' Her tone was less playful, more concerned. For Pakistanis, family, not the individual, was the centre of everything.

Uncle Tier encouraged me to go. He saw *me*, not just the person I was supposed to be. 'You need to live life, this is what it's about, son! You'll have a great time. You got a 2:1, you can celebrate, especially if you're not even paying for it!' A law firm had given me £500 just for being on Oxford's Law with European Law course and I had told him I was considering using the money on a last-minute trip to Thailand.

'So this Clare then, just you and her going, yeah? Is she a friend or a *friend* friend? Come on, son, I won't tell your mum,' he teased on the phone. I laughed it off, purposefully not answering so as to let him wonder. I considered lying to my parents about the fact that she and I were going alone, but it was no bad thing for them to worry she was my girlfriend even though I assured them she was not.

I sat on the sand, picking at shells and rocks, examining them briefly before throwing them towards the dunes. I thought of our flight over here. Across the aisle sat an elderly couple. He wore a blue cap, short-sleeved turquoise shirt and jeans. Her old hands were decorated with pink nail varnish and gold jewellery. As we took off, she clutched his arm in panic and nestled her head in his chest. I watched them. She was soothed by his presence. Watching them made me want my own person to hold on to.

I stared at the rock in my palm. It was ivory in colour and the size of a Brazil nut. Its curves gave it the shape of a human heart, with a perfectly round hole formed in the middle. I decided to keep it and have it turned into a necklace. One day, I would give it to the person I married. To show her that I thought of her at the inception of my adult life and willed her into being. Then I let myself adjust the picture, turning *her* into *him*, the necklace at *his* throat. My mind was a prison but it was also the only place where I was free. I'd propose with the necklace, telling him the story behind it. He'd say *yes* and the wedding would be huge and colourful. A seven-day Pakistani extravaganza with a henna ceremony. Matching grooms in complementary traditional Pakistani attire.

The cracks were beginning to appear in my mental resolve and through them my imagination slipped in, taking me down deeper tunnels. Dark tunnels that led to places filled with light. But it would never be real, because even if I could picture being with a man, I could never imagine my family by my side. Their son marrying a man was unthinkable but a wedding without my parents was to me like the sky without its blue.

The crashing waves made a soothing sound. The palm trees at the edge of the beach swayed. Staring at them now, I couldn't imagine being scared of them. These trees were too beautiful to house jinn. I was an adult and had to let go of the bogeyman of my childhood. With a jolt of self-awareness I saw jinn for what they really were, a fiction that had lived inside me for years, that I had used to hide behind, to explain away the things that were too difficult to accept. I needed to face up to the reality that these sexual feelings belonged not to some little demon spirit but to me. I wasn't possessed and, although it was difficult to acknowledge, I never had been. I was gay.

'MOZZA, over here!' Clare stood between the hut and the dance floor made of sand. She rocked from side to side gesturing for me to join in. An electricity seemed to pulse through the dancers. Young, bare, sun-kissed bodies fuelled by alcohol and other substances. But even dancing didn't help with this mood that cast a shadow over the sunshine of my holiday.

'That giirrrll won't stop asking about you.' Clare was slurring a little.

'I'm not interested,' I said.

'Come on, Mozza, cheer up. What's wrong? You've been a misery guts since we arrived! She's gorgeous! Why the bloody hell won't you go for it?'

'I ... I ... well ... I've never kissed anyone before.' I blurted it out. It was the truth. Not strictly relevant but the best answer I could come up with.

'What? Come here!' Clare shouted before grabbing my head and pulling me in. Her lips did most of the work; mine were frozen solid with shock.

'Now off you go.' She patted me on the bum before wandering into the crowd.

I felt trapped in a room with only one escape route. I found the slim Dutch girl. We climbed up a sand dune overlooking the party. My attempts to fill the silence with small talk about the fact I'd be moving to Holland the year after next were cut short by her hand touching my face as she moved closer. We kissed and kissed and kissed. It was a strange sensation. Sensual, but more in a nice long bath sort of way than erotic. I wondered when I could stop. How much kissing would it take to prove to her, to Clare and to myself that I was a real man? Her hand moved to my chest. Where was this going? It continued to move slowly down. My hands were behind me and I began clutching for something to hold on to but the sand just slipped through my fingers. She was about to reach my crotch. If she did, the game would be up. I'd be rumbled. In one rapid movement, I pushed her away and leapt to my feet. She looked upset. 'I … I'm sorry … I just can't … I'm Muslim,' I said before darting down the dune to find Clare.

Instead I found Danielle, the sister of a friend of ours from Keble who, by some random coincidence, happened to be in the same country, at the same party. We'd said hi to her and her girlfriend earlier.

'Have you seen Clare?' I asked.

'Yeah, I think I saw her with some guy. They headed that way but they'll be back soon. Don't worry, you can join us. Are you OK?'

'Yeah … yeah, I'm fine, I'm just …' I wanted to say 'tearful'. 'Lonely'. 'Lost'.

'Do you want to sit down for a sec?' Danielle asked, pointing at the sand. Her family was Jewish, I knew, because her brother had told me. The Jewish people I'd met seemed to understand the Muslim family dynamic better than most.

'What's wrong?' Danielle was practically a stranger and yet I felt a solidarity with her.

'Your parents know you're gay, right?' I asked.

'Yeah.'

'I have this friend. She's Muslim,' I said. 'But she's a lesbian.'

'Oh. Wow, OK.'

'She doesn't know what to do. She's told me but no one else. I really want to help her but I don't know how. Sometimes I feel like I can't even reach her, like she's there but she's ignoring me. How do I help her?'

'Well ...' Danielle paused for a moment. 'I think the best thing you can do is listen.'

'Should she tell anyone?'

'Apart from you, you mean?' she said.

'Sorry, yes, I mean apart from me.'

'Well, only she can decide that. For me, telling the first person was the hardest and then it just sort of snowballed from there and before I knew it I was a card-carrying lesbian.' She smiled. 'It just kind of figured itself out, you know?' I longed for a world in which things just figured themselves out.

19

As the summer of 2004 drew to an end, I thought more and more about those young people enjoying themselves on the beach, about how distant I felt from them, from the lightness of their lives. For me, everything felt heavy. I became lethargic.

My parents insisted on a third pilgrimage to Damascus before the start of my second year but returning to Syria made me feel uneasy. If I had to go back, I was taking my heart necklace with me.

The summer air in Damascus was uncomfortably close, suffocating almost. As I walked into the now familiar shrine, my shoulders hunched as my heart shrank. A wave of doubt and disappointment flooded through me and began to overflow. I moved to a space against the back wall and lowered myself to the ground, shrouded in a crowd of pilgrims. I cushioned my head between my knees. I wondered whether God could hear me, whether he had heard me all these years and had chosen not to listen. Or whether he couldn't hear me at all.

I kneeled and brought my hands together, cupped in prayer, and raised them up towards the ceiling of the dome. The call to prayer began ringing out over the dusty city. Islam felt like a rope to which I had clung. Over the last few years the rope had frayed. I'd held on to the words of God, 'Call upon Me; I will respond to you', but they hadn't changed a thing.

Here in the mosque, the same place I had sat twice before, I began once again to ask for a cure. But the words I had repeated five times a day since the age of thirteen refused to come. I'd said some 11,000 prayers and I couldn't do it any more. I walked out of the shrine, realising there was nothing left for me in there. I felt suddenly untethered and adrift.

Back in London, my friends and I started the night in a West End bar. It was the last week of holidays and a few of us had decided to have a night out before second year got under way.

'You're the London boy, Mos. Any ideas of where next?' Paul asked as he, Sophie and Layla all turned to me. The four of us stood underneath a brick railway arch outside the entrance to the club. An urgent thought flickered. I was reminded of the walks I'd taken through Soho after my shifts on Oxford Street. G-A-Y? No, I couldn't suggest a bar actually called 'Gay'. There was another, I recalled. Down a side street that wasn't fronted by drag queens and had no rainbow flags outside.

'I know one place but I don't know if it's any good.' I rubbed the back of my neck, speaking nonchalantly to moderate any hint of desperation in my tone. But I was desperate.

Layla shrugged in approval.

'Sounds good to me,' Paul said.

'Yeah, let's do it. I'm not ready to call it a night,' Sophie added.

On the way to Soho I scrambled to remember where the place was. I had to find it. I couldn't risk getting within touching distance of this experience, only for it to slip away. I didn't want to go to a gay club. I needed to. I needed to see what it was like inside, what I was like inside it.

I pointed indifferently towards the red velvet rope guarding the double doors of a club I thought might be the one I was looking for. 'What about that one?'

'You know this is a gay club, right, guys?' the bouncer said.

'Oh! Er ...' I looked at the others.

'I don't care. Let's go,' Sophie said, ushering us in before I could feign protest.

Walking through a mirrored corridor, then down two flights of stairs, towards the muffled sound of Michael and Janet Jackson's 'Scream', my senses became heightened. I had goose bumps. My pupils danced in the darkness and strobe lighting. I wanted to hold Layla's hand but I had to do this alone.

'You guys go get drinks, I'll come and find you at the bar, I just need the loo,' I said. As they walked away, I closed my eyes and took a deep breath. And then another. I opened them. The room was oval, with a dance floor cordoned off in the middle. The bar was at one end, and I at the other. Men everywhere. Attractive men everywhere. Attractive, gay men everywhere. I needed to look at all of them but I couldn't look at any. I fought the urge to rush after the others, to hide in the safety of the group. I forced myself to take it all in. I could feel eyes on me, on my face and my legs and from behind. I turned to meet them, one by one, before looking back at the dance floor. Then I saw him. He was standing in the middle with two others. Handsome, white. I wondered what his world looked like. I wanted to follow it. To peer inside. I envied it. I wanted it. I wanted him.

'Hi ... you aren't very subtle,' he said, leaning in so that I might hear him over the music. His breath on my neck made my skin tingle, as if I'd been thrown from hot water into freezing cold. My legs felt weak. Did men kiss the same way normal people did? My lips quivered. I imagined the devil standing behind me, pushing me towards this beautiful man. He was close enough that I could see his pores. Close enough to see the faint frown lines. To see that his lips were warm and pink and smooth. My mouth was dry. My mind so vivid with images it was empty of words. I pushed past him, escaped the dance floor and found the others.

'Are you OK?' Layla asked.

'No, I'm ... I mean ... yeah. I just, I think I have a funny tummy or something.'

'Oh shit! Shall I tell Paul not to bother with drinks?'

'No, it's OK, you guys have one and then we'll go?'

I stood next to them, my back to the dance floor. They were my shelter from all the things I desperately wanted but equally feared.

After the club, we returned to the London town house we were staying in together, belonging to a friend's parents who were on holiday. The others fell asleep quickly in the room we shared but I was wide awake and feeling distraught. The clock read 4 a.m. and I got up, worried I might wake them if I got emotional.

Layla had been watching and followed me, finding me head in arms, on the cold tiles of the bathroom floor. I hadn't realised how much I was panting until she told me. I couldn't catch my breath.

'It's OK.' Layla reached over to hold my hand but I pulled it away. No one could reach me now. She closed the door and sat against it.

'You've not been yourself for a while. I've noticed and the others have too,' she said.

'Keep it down,' I whispered. Paul and Sophie were asleep next door.

'You've been quiet all evening.'

'You know that the Prophet Muhammed once said, "Speak the truth even if it is against yourself"?'

'Er ... OK ...'

'And that "the path to hell is paved with lies"?'

'Listen, Mohsin, I know your faith is important to you, but you never actually talk about it. What's going on? What happened in Syria?'

'Syria?'

'Yes, Syria. Since you've been back you've been different.' She was right. In Damascus something had shifted. It was as though I had been emptied of all spirituality.

'I'm a liar,' I said. I couldn't look at her.

'Ok ...'

'I'm not a good person. I've tried to be but I'm just not. I've lied to everyone. And I'll keep lying because I have no other choice.'

'Mohsin, what's wrong?'

'Would you still want to be friends with me if you knew I'd done something awful?' I met her eyes for the first time.

'Erm ... what do you mean?'

'If I was evil, truly evil, would you still want to be friends with me?'

'Well, no, I guess if you were truly evil I probably wouldn't,' she said slowly. 'But I think I know you well enough by now. Just tell me.' I turned away. 'Is it something you've done? Something at your old school? Whatever it was, I'm sure you've learned your lesson. I'm not going to judge you for it. Have you ... killed someone?'

'Bloody hell! No!' I said, laughing a little longer than I should have.

'Well, what am I supposed to think? You won't tell me!' She leaned over and poked me.

'I'm ... I'm ...' I paused. She squeezed my hand.

I was starting to feel nauseous. Out of the bathroom window my eyes fixed onto a lone star. It shone so brightly, all by itself in the night-time sky. I became hypnotised by its aloneness. I knew that somehow, by living this half-life of mine, I had jettisoned the most important part of *me*. I had abandoned the little boy I had once been, full of possibility and feeling. He'd been banished to the prison of my own making. Wherever he was right now, it felt like he was looking at that star too. As if for the first time since parting ways, we had been reunited. A surge of hope came over me. It might not be too late to save him. It was startling how real he suddenly was and how important it felt to find my way back to him. He was a little boy, crouched on the ground, his arms wrapped around his knees, in a damp, cold room. He wore shorts the same shade of green as the Pakistan flag. It was painful to reflect on how badly I had treated him, the hatred I had shown him.

When he'd tried to whisper to me I'd slapped him down. When he'd sought my attention I'd called him a jinn, or the devil, I hated myself that much. The boy had wounds that had dried and scarred. Wounds that kept healing because he refused to die, because his life force was stronger than mine, because he was made of the truth. Any light in my life came from him. I offered my hand. I would not mistreat him any more. He took it. I told him I was scared too.

'Layla ...' I guided him out of the dungeon and brought him into the world and set him free. 'I'm gay.'

20

'All that's left for me to say now is, again, welcome to Keble. Please stick around for some drinks and an ice-breaker session,' I told two hundred first years in my role as college president. Returning to Oxford for my second year was about escaping my parents, rather than realising academic ambition; this felt very clear. I was so far away from them now I wasn't sure I'd ever make it back. The path behind me was light years away and the one in front uncharted.

'Salaam. It's Mohsin, right? I'm Hamza.' A fresher from Newcastle, Hamza was studying economics and management. We were standing at the entrance to the grand dining hall.

'Wasalaam, Hamza. Welcome to Keble,' I said, his hand clasped between both of mine.

'Honestly, I'm so pleased to meet you. When I read the welcome brochure and saw your picture, I guessed you were Muslim. Why did you sign your name "Mos"?'

'Ah, actually I did sign off with my name but the editors changed it.'

'Seriously?'

'Yeah, it's no big deal, got to make it a bit easier for these *goreh*, you know?'

'Also thank you so much for the halal food.'

My stomach tied itself in a knot. He was trying to bond with me over religion, but my faith was in pieces; more and more of it falling away with each day that passed.

'How did you make that happen?' His enthusiasm reminded me of myself a year ago.

'I asked for it,' I said. I'd made life a little easier for Keble's Muslim students, just as I was coming to accept I might no longer be one of them.

'I've never been this happy!' I screamed before laughing uncontrollably. I felt like I'd taken some magical potion that made each of my nerve endings buzz. I was stooped in the old wooden doorway of a nearby Oxford college. Layla and others stood around me, sober, a mixture of concern and puzzlement showing on their faces.

'It's OK, guys, I'm fine. Why the sad faces?! I'm finally drinking! You always wanted me to and now ... and now ... and now I'm going to the Bridge, I want to DANCE,' I shouted, starting to shimmy.

'It's closed, Mos, it's not even 8 p.m. yet. Let's go back to college, OK? You can dance in your room,' one of them said.

'How did he get like this?' Ish asked.

'He said he wanted to try it, but in private,' Layla explained. 'So we went to my room. Then Amy knocked on my door and wanted to talk to me, she was upset, so I told him to wait while I spoke to her in the corridor. She's just broken up with her boyfriend so I couldn't just tell her to go away. He must have started drinking the minute I left the room.' She let out a long sigh.

'Well, now the whole fucking college has seen him drunk at 7 p.m.,' Ish said.

'I didn't mean for that to happen!' Layla said.

'Guys, GUYS! Guys, I'm fine. FINE! I've been sooooo, sooooo sad, but it's OK now. It's all over. I get it!'

'What does he mean?'

'He's just drunk, ignore him,' Layla said anxiously.

'Stop fighting, Mos!' Ish tussled with me but I broke free and with a burst of energy made off towards the club.

'You're hot ... I'd pull you ... you are fit!' I was pointing at random strangers. My drunken shadow lurched and lunged until the group caught up with me and Nick grabbed me. My devoted friends chased me through the streets of Oxford, knowing I couldn't be left alone. The thrill of the chase ignited another burst of energy and I ran into the middle of a main road. I could see the bus coming towards me.

'GET OUT OF THE ROAD, MOS!' shouts came from behind. I should just let it hit me.

When Layla had asked me if I was sure about trying alcohol, I didn't know because I wasn't sure of anything any more, aside from my anger. Angry enough to prove to myself that I didn't need religion. I longed to touch and to be touched. Without human contact I was cut off from the world. I laughed as the bus came closer, its bright colours flickering intermittently as it passed under street lamps.

Someone grabbed me and shoved me to the side. The bus went by as I fell to the ground still laughing uncontrollably.

BANG! I felt a smack on my head. BANG! Another.

'OW!'

'Sophie! Hold the fucking seat up!' Layla shouted.

'Sorry, I just, I just ... sorry, I just can't believe the state he's in.' Layla's toilet reeked of vomit. I couldn't stop retching even though by now my stomach was empty. It was as if my body was trying to eject the emptiness inside my heart. I wondered whether this was the exorcism I'd been waiting for all along.

Later, when I opened my eyes again, my surroundings were shifting from side to side, like I was on a treacherous sea crossing. The curtains were drawn but the midday sun fought through, illuminating dust particles that floated slowly in the air. The butterfly fairy lights over the bed made me feel safe. Layla was asleep on the floor, I in her bed. I welled up, unable to move, unable to comprehend what I had done. I turned over, closed my eyes and made myself as small as I could.

I woke again with a clanging headache. Layla was beside me.

'Drink this,' she said. 'It will help.'

'Why is the bed so wet?' I asked, sitting up and leaning against the wall.

'You were sweating a lot. Seemed like you might have been having nightmares from some of the sounds you were making.'

'I'm so sexy.' I smiled at her and she gave me a weak smile back.

'You need to see someone,' she said. I said nothing, too embarrassed to ask what had happened – I had some flashbacks but not the full picture of my crazy night.

'You nearly got yourself killed and it seemed like you didn't even care.'

'I had my first ever drink, Layla – of course I was going to react strangely.'

'It's not just that. You said some horrible things. Horrible things about yourself, about the way you feel. The others heard it too.'

I thought I might be sick again. 'Did I ... ?'

'No, you didn't. I thought you might on a couple of occasions and I interrupted, but it's weird, you were totally out of control, and yet something inside you knew to keep your secret even in that terrible state. I'm sorry.'

'It's not your fault.'

'But what happened? I only left you alone for twenty minutes.'

'Well, I was waiting and then I just picked up that bottle and drank.' I pointed to the empty bottle of arak on the floor.

'You drank that straight?!'

I nodded.

'And you didn't think it was disgusting?'

'Of course. It tasted like acid but I thought I was having that reaction because I wasn't used to it. I guess I wasn't supposed to?'

'Why didn't you wait for me?'

'I was tired of waiting and I wanted a release, to just tune everything out, you know?' Isolation and shame was a poisonous cocktail. I looked up at the ceiling and closed my eyes.

My fears about the devil, my family, my faith and myself all dissolved in my alcohol-soaked brain. I was outside my parents' house, but they couldn't find me like this, on my knees. I grabbed the handle of the front door and levered myself to my feet. I crept slowly up the carpeted staircase, holding my breath as tightly as I held on to the banisters. I stumbled into my room, collapsing into giggles on the carpet. A light came on.

'Mochie?'

I looked up at the bed in the centre of the room to see my mum and dad, staring down at me in confusion. I was not in my own room, but theirs. The disgust on their faces told me they could smell the stench of alcohol.

'I'm fine, I'm fine, I'm not hurt, don't worry,' I slurred, struggling to my feet. I reached into the pocket of my jeans and a condom packet fell out and onto their bed. I looked at it and then at them. My mum began to scream and so did I. I woke up alone in Layla's room screaming, soaked in sweat. I hugged the pillow, hoping that it would absorb the guilt about what I had done and what I might do next.

21

'WHITE BOY!' someone shouted as I crossed the college quad. The slur had been yelled from a window. I looked up and confirmed it had come from Hamza's room. The same slight that had been used against me at school but for different reasons. I couldn't blame him. From the outside, and perhaps the inside too, that is what I had become. The person he had met was a teetotal Muslim who campaigned for halal food. The person he saw stumbling around the college was a drinker who had stopped praying. I was already so ashamed of myself that his words were but a drop in a cesspool of self-loathing.

Now that I was no longer praying five times a day I caught myself crying at odd moments, dazed by the feeling that something was missing. I longed for the peace and stability that my faith had once brought me but I couldn't find it there. I'd programmed myself to hate the person I was. It felt like the only way to let go of the hate was to let go of the faith I had tied it to.

Ramadan, the month of fasting, had arrived, and on day one I couldn't bring myself to fast. It was the first one I'd missed in years. On day two, I woke up early but after laying out the prayer mat I found myself just staring at it as the sun slowly rose. By day three I had stopped pretending to myself that I could do it. But the drinking and the not fasting weren't enough. I was angry and I cast around for a single, roaring act of defiance.

The thunderous Sunday sky told the little boy inside me that God was angry. I made no attempt to protect myself from the rain that fell in torrents onto the Oxford streets, as I scurried from restaurant to restaurant searching for something very special on the menus posted in windows. And then, there it was: gammon steak.

I took a seat as far away from the window as possible; I wanted no witnesses. As I hunched over the menu, I thought of the slouched, solitary man drinking in Edward Hopper's *Nighthawks*. Although until only very recently I hadn't been one of them, plenty of young Muslims drank and took drugs. Pork, however, was the final frontier, the word alone enough to make the skin of even the most relaxed worshipper crawl. Pork was my final *fuck you* to any part of me that still believed. After ordering, I double-checked with the waiter that it was indeed pork. Raindrops dripped from my hair onto the checked tablecloth. As a child, I hadn't been allowed to say the word 'pig'. Instead we spelled it out, 'P-I-G'. When I first saw the sign for 'G-A-Y' I wondered whether it had been named in the same vein. And yet here I was about to eat it. Pig, pig, pig.

As the waiter set the plate down in front of me, I imagined the razor-sharp edges of the bright red line I was about to cross. The smell, which reminded me of rotten egg, made me want to heave. The white border of fat framed the pink fleshy meat. I poked at it, half expecting it to lunge back. I glanced around uneasily, imagining the eyes of the other people in the restaurant focused on me and my pig steak.

'Is everything OK, sir?' the waiter asked.

'Yes, yes. Fine. Thank you.' At least ten minutes had passed and I hadn't touched it.

'Would you prefer something else?'

'No, no. I'm good.' I had to do this. I had to. With a burst of resolve, as if I were about to jump willingly into ice-cold water, I grabbed the knife and fork, cut off a small piece of reddish meat and put in my mouth.

I gagged straight away. I had hesitated so long the meat was cold. I saw someone glance over, I must have looked so strange, staring at my plate as if I hated it. But I would keep chewing. All night if I had to. After the first piece slid down my throat I gulped an entire glass of water, as if it might cleanse the sin slipping into my body. I sat back in my chair, waiting. Do not be sick, Mohsin, I told myself over and over. A few minutes later I was ready for the next bite. I wanted to speed up, to get it over with, but risked throwing up with each mouthful. I closed my eyes and swallowed piece after piece. My head hurt, but the plate was finally empty. I held back the urge to pick it up and throw it at the restaurant windows.

Soon after returning to university for my second year, I told Ish my secret. With her Sikh background, Ish knew, first-hand, how South Asian culture treated people like me.

'Oh God, Mos! You're totally fucked!' she said in her broad northern accent, a statement I found reassuring because it correlated with my own feelings about the situation. In Ish I found a family. I could go to her room at any time of day or night, sometimes to talk but also just to sleep in the comfort of her presence.

Then I told Clare, who had a slightly different reaction.

'Mozza, you have Mariah Carey's back catalogue and you didn't grope me once in Thailand, even when we shared a bed. Of course I know!' she said, wrapping her arms around me. 'Let's get you out to meet boys!'

As Clare and I approached the club, the butterflies in my stomach felt like they were on speed.

'I'm sorry. Not tonight.'

'What? What do you mean?' Clare asked with feigned surprise.

'I mean *not tonight*,' he replied.

'Look, my friend told me about this place –'

'You know it's a gay night?' He was staring at me.

'I'm a lesbian and he's with me, so can we please come in now?'

The large, dimly lit room was almost empty. I could feel the eyes of the few present linger over me.

'He's not bad, Mozza – what do you reckon?'

I hesitated. I'd spent years evaluating the attractiveness of men but always on my own. I leaned against the bar, my eyes fixed on Clare, too frightened to catch anyone else's gaze. Although I was twenty years old, coming out made me feel as though I was going through a second adolescence.

'Just gonna pop to the loo, Mozza. Back in a sec,' Clare said.

'No! I'll come with you,' I said.

'To the ladies? You might be gay, but that doesn't mean I'm gonna let you watch me pee. Stay here, maybe make some friends.'

I stared at the drink she had bought me and then at the shoes I was wearing before moving back to the drink.

'Hi, it's Mos, right?' I looked up to see Shane, one of the people who worked in Keble Hall, in a white T-shirt two sizes too small.

'Um ... no, sorry,' I said, staring at my shoes again.

'You go to Keble, don't you?' he said earnestly.

'No, I'm sorry. I don't,' I said, taking a sip of my drink, avoiding his eyes. As soon as he was far enough away I put the drink down and rushed to the men's toilets. I locked myself in a cubicle. I could see two shadows on the floor of the next cubicle, pressed up against each other, and heard the sounds of exchanging saliva followed by those of an intense sniffing, which I guessed might be some wild sexual act. I lowered the toilet lid, sat down and wrapped my arms around myself, rocking back and forth.

Don't cry. Don't cry. Don't cry. I wanted to go home. Not back to college but home, home. I wanted my mum. I wanted her to hold me and tell me I was going to be OK. I wanted to be straight, now more than ever.

Clare insisted I stay. I'd come this far and couldn't give up. 'Have another drink – that'll chill you out,' she said as she handed me a glass of vodka and Red Bull. 'Ooh, he's nice!'

I looked up and instantly locked eyes with a guy who was smiling at me. I turned back to Clare.

'And here he comes, Mozza ...'

The butterflies now felt like they were eating at my insides to get out.

'Hi,' he said.

'I'll leave you boys to it. I think I see Shane over there.'

'No! Clare –' But she had walked away.

I froze.

'You're really thirsty,' he observed as I drained my glass before ordering another.

The pounding of my heart made it difficult to speak. He stepped closer to me.

Unable to take my eyes off him, I felt simultaneously repulsed and excited. A slim silver chain hung at his neck; his navy shirt complemented his Mediterranean skin. He took my hand in his and I flinched. As he pulled me closer, his musky scent danced slowly around me, and the music seemed euphoric. As our lips met, I exhaled, and with the release of my breath something else escaped too: I had let go. My body tingled. I'd never felt more myself, a feeling completely foreign to me until that moment. He gently put his hand on the side of my neck. His movements became more frequent and passionate. I was overwhelmed.

'God, you're amazing,' he whispered in my ear before kissing my neck.

What was I doing? I pushed him away and ran for the exit, leaving Clare behind. The release I had felt only moments ago was gone. As I emerged from the club, the world waiting for me outside seemed unrecognisable. It was black with the darkness of night-time and bitingly cold and I feared it might always be this way.

22

'Mozza! It's only the most famous, or should I say infamous, party in Oxford. Come on, what could be more fun than watching dressed-up poshos get wankered?' Clare had a spare ticket to the Piers Gaveston ball, an annual event organised by the elite of the elite at Oxford. 'Just wear all black, you don't have to get your buns out, although I'm sure the boys would love it!'

Ball was the generous description for what was essentially a few tents in a field on the outskirts of the city. Tents filled with scantily clad, irreverent men and women fuelled by alcohol and drugs. Drugs like the little red Ecstasy pill I held in my hand. The trance and techno beats were unforgiving and bounced my attempts to reason from side to side. I had lost Clare. A short topless girl, in gold body paint and large black nipple tassels, danced over to me and tried, unsuccessfully, to put the pill in my mouth. A boy in stiletto heels, red glittery hot pants, and a black cape held in place by a studded dog collar smacked my bum with his whip and winked at me as he strutted out of the tent to the glowing bonfire outside. This is what hell might actually look like. It was certainly the thing of nightmares for my parents, if their imaginations could even stretch to it. Whereas these partygoers needed fancy dress to bring them closer to debauched ungodliness, my very existence did it for me.

On a large screen at the back of the tent there appeared to be a man and woman having sex. I stared at the flickering images, unable to avert my gaze until a very tall woman blocked my view. She wore a corset and gold leggings, and moved towards me smiling. She leaned in and I pushed her away.

'Oh, come on,' she said.

'No! No ... I don't like women,' I mumbled.

'What?'

'I don't like women,' I repeated. She removed her wig. Her hair was short. A boy! He leaned in again.

'No, you have make-up on,' I said.

'It's only a bit of make-up,' he said, grabbing my hips, but I pushed him away again. I'd grown up with a firm idea of what a man should and should not be, which I couldn't shake even then. After he walked away, I danced by myself to techno music that sounded like one long track.

Trays of food hovered, arms reaching out to grab small handfuls before sharing their indiscernible contents with those nearby. I saw they were mushrooms, piled on top of each other. I was hungry so took some and was about to pop one in my mouth when my hand was slapped away.

'Mozza, no! Those are magic mushrooms! No drugs for you, my friend. I don't think it's wise given the mood you've been in recently,' Clare shouted over the music. She took the mushrooms from my hand and threw them on the floor. 'Are you OK?'

I nodded and giggled.

'You're not, are you?'

'I feel great!' I raised my arms, and began to dance.

'Come with me. Let's get you some water.'

It was only when I woke up the next morning that I realised how far I had fallen. How reckless I was becoming and how little it bothered me.

*

Layla and I sat on the fraying red, velvet cinema seats with a box of popcorn. We'd heard that *Ae Fond Kiss*, the new Ken Loach film, had an Egyptian main character.

In fact it transpired that the film was a downbeat story about a Scottish Pakistani who is due to marry his cousin when he falls in love with an Irish Catholic woman. The film dealt with the destruction their love wreaked on his family.

'Shall we leave?' Layla whispered. Tears rolled down my cheeks as the father pleaded with his son not to put the family through such pain. We left before the lights came up.

'Just give me a second,' I said, as we stood outside the old cinema. The gravity of my predicament had never escaped me but watching the scenario unfold on screen felt like I'd been punched in the gut by a wrecking ball. Walking away from the cinema, I turned down a side street and asked Layla not to follow me. When I got far enough away that I didn't think she could see, I dropped to my knees and folded into myself. I lowered my head to the pavement, sobbing. Layla was there in an instant, wrapping her arms around my shaking body.

'What am I going to do? What am I going to do?' I repeated over and over as she clung on, refusing to let go.

Later that evening, after I had reassured her that I would go straight to bed, I went for a walk, pausing at the broad steps of the main entrance to Keble chapel. The ten-foot doors were recessed, creating an enclave draped in shadow. I huddled into it and looked up at the night sky. The stone gargoyles glared at me disapprovingly. Across the quad, I saw figures skipping home from drunken nights out without, it seemed, a care in the world. I envied them. The idea of ending my own life had begun sneaking into my thoughts.

'I knew I'd find you here.' Ish loomed into view. 'Layla told me what happened. Come on, you can't stay here.' She joined me, putting her arms around me. 'You're two different people at the moment, Mos. One minute you're Mr President and the next you're sitting out here in the shadows by yourself ... I want my best mate back. We need to get you some help.'

A few days later I made my way to the college nurses' office. My thoughts were plunging ever deeper into a dark and terrifying place, the nightmares more vivid than ever. I reasoned the nurse could prescribe some sleeping pills.

'The over-the-counter tablets aren't really working any more. I've tried taking four or five but still nothing,' I explained to the nurse. The kindness in her eyes put me at ease.

'When was the last time you got a good night's sleep without pills or alcohol?' she asked.

I didn't know the answer. To stop themselves from drowning, dolphins only ever allow half their brain to sleep at any one time, never fully switching off. My mind was operating in much the same way, half awake, trying not to sink. Sleeping pills were the only way to turn off completely.

'Well, for a start, you must stop taking so many pills, that's dangerous. I can't just give you stronger medication. Can you tell me why you aren't sleeping?' I was silent for a while.

'I'm gay and it's a problem, so I think about it a lot and it makes it hard to sleep. I'm just so tired all the time and that's no good, I need to work,' I said. I just needed the damn tablets. She took a deep breath.

'Mohsin, I'm not sure that sleeping pills are what you need.'

'No, honestly, *they are*. Please.' I was desperate.

'You need support,' she said.

Earlier that week, I had taken the bus to London after reading about a youth LGBT support group. I paced back and forth outside the door tucked away in a side street behind Piccadilly Circus. After finally plucking up the courage to go inside, I walked into a room empty but for the two youth workers. They greeted me like the first customer of the day. I was too disappointed to open up but it would have been rude to leave straight away, so I sat down exchanging polite conversation for forty minutes before taking the bus straight back to Oxford.

'I do talk to people. I talk to my friends about it but that doesn't help me sleep.'

'I mean specialist support, I mean a therapist.' As if I couldn't be any more Western, the nurse was now suggesting I talk to a stranger about my problems. The idea made me deeply uncomfortable but I also knew that it wasn't normal to think often about life coming to an end.

The counselling service was located in an affluent part of the city, on an old Oxford square lined with terraced houses circling a public garden. A desk was tucked to one side of the room, leaving space for two wing-backed armchairs in the middle, separated by a small table on which, somewhat stereotypically, sat a box of tissues. Maureen was American, which gave this already disconcerting experience a cinematic quality. Softly spoken yet assured, her words were surprisingly firm and disarming at the same time. I wanted to dislike her, to resist letting it all out and her in.

'I'm gay but I'm not sure why I'm here because I know there's nothing you can do to help me,' I said, as a matter of fact. She wasn't Muslim. How could she understand? But would I ever find a Muslim who might?

'If by that you mean that I can't make you straight, then I suppose you're right,' she said. 'But would you like to tell me about it?' She was relaxed, encouraging me to feel the same. Taking a deep breath, I attempted to explain.

'Well, I'm Muslim … and I'm gay.' I thought God would be less angry if I said it in that order. I'd never had to assert both facts aloud together before.

I wasn't sure which version of me was meant to be in the room with her. Adopting a persona depending on the audience was second nature to me. She wanted to see the real me but there was no such thing. Instead of being a complete person, I was a collection of broken parts.

'To be honest, I'm not sure there's much to say. I don't think there's anything you can do to help. I've thought about this a lot, every which way. There is no solution, every path leads to a dead end.'

'What do you mean by that?'

I paused for a moment, wincing at the idea of using a Gwyneth Paltrow romcom as an analogy to illustrate something so uncomfortable.

'Have you seen the film *Sliding Doors*?' I asked.

'I think so, but remind me.'

'Basically the story follows a woman's life as it splits in two. In one version she catches a train home and discovers that her boyfriend is having an affair. In the alternative life she misses the train and doesn't uncover the adultery, at least not straight away.'

'OK,' she said evenly.

'Well, I often think about how the different versions of my life might play out depending on whether I tell my family or not.'

'So tell me what happens in each version.'

'Well, if I come out my family is going to be devastated. They'll be shunned by their community and by other parts of our family too. My parents might stop talking to me and I don't know what my brothers will do but maybe they won't be allowed to talk to me either. And they might find it harder to find people to marry. I'm not sure they'll ever be able to cope with it.'

'What about you?' she asked gently.

'What?'

'What happens to you in that scenario?'

'I'll be alone. I won't have them any more. I guess I'll meet a few guys here and there but ultimately I'll end up alone because I'll never be able to replace my family. I'll never find anyone who understands my situation. And my career will suffer. And what if I get HIV?'

'Why do you think your career will suffer?'

'Because there is so much homophobia in society. People think it's OK because we're in 2004 but things are still really bad. The other day, this guy in college said if one of his friends came out he'd stop talking to them, and he's white!'

'What about the alternative life, the one in which you don't come out?'

'If I get married and have kids I'll be miserable but everyone else will be happy. I'm bound to cheat, to have affairs, and I don't want that. How can I marry someone in good conscience knowing that I'm treating her life as a shield for mine? I can't do that to another human being,' I said, shaking my head. 'And what do I get if I just stick to the rules and don't act on my desires? According to some it's forty virgins – females of course. That's the very last thing I want, so what's the point?' I smiled, but it was a serious question. If I decided to respect the rules, would I go to heaven and wake up straight? And if I did, would I cease to be me?

'Maybe you're protecting yourself from the possibility of a fulfilled gay relationship because if you were to acknowledge that this was possible you would find it unbearable to give it up,' she said. Such a simple observation that immediately got to the heart of it.

'Do you think you can feel nostalgic for a life you will never live?' I asked, sitting back in my chair. 'I imagine I will spend my life daydreaming about the one I could have had, in some alternative universe, where none of this matters.'

'What does the life that you say you will never live look like?'

'It's sunny because I hate the cold.' I grinned. 'Have you seen *Will & Grace*?'

'Yes.'

'My mum's the one who introduced me to it. She thinks it's really funny. Their lives seem so uncomplicated by their sexuality. I know it's TV but there must be people out there like that. Who just lead normal lives and happen to be gay. On the one hand I love it because I get to see how easy it is for them, but on the other I can't ever picture it being that way for me and it hurts. The show definitely makes me feel less lonely though. It's like my gay best friend.'

I considered her question again.

'I guess in this other life I have a partner and I can be with him without shame. In that world, my parents love him like a son and embrace him like they would my wife. My brothers love him too and we can all go out for meals together and go on holiday and just ... just be a family that loves each other.'

'Do you think that's too much to ask?' she said.

'To ask of whom? There's no one listening to me any more.'

'You don't think God listens to you?'

'How could any God have done this to me? A just God would have heard me over the last seven years.' I was pleading now, but with whom it was unclear. 'I prayed five times a day and asked for one simple thing each time.' Thousands of prayers to be cured gone unanswered. I was breathing harder now, caught up in my anger. 'We believe life is a test but if God is all-knowing then what is the point because he knows what choices you're going to make before you've made them, before you're even born! AND THIS IS NO CHOICE!'

23

The sun had begun to stir in the dawn sky. The landline in my room rang.

'Hello?'

'Mohsin, it's me. It's your dad, he's been arrested!' my mum said before bursting into tears.

'What? What's happened?' I asked frantically, checking the time on my mobile. It was almost 6 a.m. and I had dozens of missed calls.

'They burst in, so many of them. Police officers,' she said through sobs. 'They've taken him away.'

'Where, Mum? Where have they taken him?'

'There's been some sort of fraud at the post office ... he's at the police station. They wouldn't tell us anything.'

Before leaving for London, I wrote to my college tutor explaining all the facts as I knew them and told him that I was returning home for a few days. Although I was overwhelmed with concern for my dad, I couldn't help but worry about the impression this would make. I was feeding the stereotype of an Asian from the ghetto. I feared the public perception that my dad was naturally guilty because of his background, while I *knew* he was innocent. Not because he was my dad but because of the way he had raised us. On the bus back to London, I recalled countless examples of him telling us we must never cheat or take short-cuts. I'd once thought about telling the insurance company my phone was broken, so that I could get an upgrade. 'You are Pakistani. People expect you to behave like a criminal. You mustn't, this is not our country.

If you do well, you will be one of them, but if you break their rules, you are a Pakistani,' he told me.

My dad returned home shortly after I arrived. I'd never seen the look of total surrender in his eyes before. He was broken, humiliated by the experience. The thought of him being locked in a prison cell, even for a few hours, made my heart ache. During the dawn raid, they had searched the house but overlooked the shed. 'I made them search that too,' he said. 'I insisted they look everywhere. They said they wouldn't look under your little brother's bed while he slept but I told them to go ahead.'

'That's good, Dad,' I said.

'They told me, you have the right to a lawyer, and I told them no, I don't need one, I'm innocent, I'll tell you whatever you want right now.'

'What?' You didn't need to be a law student to know you always speak to a lawyer. 'Dad, were you interviewed by them?'

'Yes.'

'Without a lawyer? Why?'

'Listen! Just because you are at Oxford, it doesn't mean you are better than us. OK?' he said, mistaking my concern for loftiness.

The atmosphere was suffocating, like we were trapped in a cell. He was suspended without pay pending the outcome of the investigation, leaving the family to survive on Mum's teaching salary, with two sons at university and a mortgage.

I told my mum I was going for a walk in nearby Epping Forest. I was distraught but when I was with them I felt paralysed, unable to show pain. My family thought Oxford was changing me and they were right. I had started to think and feel in different ways. To them, however, it wasn't my thoughts or feelings they found unfamiliar but my lack of heart. Out of earshot from the house I pulled out my phone and sent a text. I'd arranged to speak to Maureen by phone instead of our usual face-to-face. She called me back just as I entered the woods. A short path between the trees led to a clearing in which an arrangement of logs had been placed around a makeshift bonfire area. I took a seat and, transfixed by the ashes from a recent fire scattering in the breeze, I recounted, without emotion, the events of the last few days.

'And how are you feeling?' she asked.

I was feeling like this was all too much, like I didn't have the mental resources to support them, to support anyone. Like it was my fault. God was sending me a clear message that to indulge my evil side was to feel his wrath. Maureen spent the rest of the call listening to me whimper among the trees.

I told my family I had no choice but to return to university. I wasn't lying but the truth was I couldn't wait to get away. Every moment at home I felt excruciating pangs of guilt. My dad wandering around the house, taunted by the spectacle of being arrested. My mum trying her best to hold things together, looking to me for support and comfort but finding none. To be present at all, I had to cut myself off from their needs, meeting them only with logic and reason.

It was soon confirmed that there was evidence of fraud committed at my dad's post office and I held my breath in the proceeding weeks, anticipating the charge that I feared would follow. If he were charged, I'd have to cancel my year abroad to Holland. Maybe leave university altogether and return home.

I was back in Oxford preparing for the president's annual black-tie dinner, an event hosted by me for three hundred people in Keble Hall. It was an opportunity for the college president to bring the students together and celebrate the community. Nothing made me feel more of a fraud than wearing a tuxedo and bow tie. They belonged to a class of wealth and power to which I did not.

On the eve of the dinner, my dad was fully exonerated of wrongdoing and his job reinstated. Bank accounts and other evidence proved that an employee had colluded with organised criminal gangs in a sophisticated and all but undetectable post office scam. He wept with relief down the phone and I wanted to be there for him. Instead I was here, at Oxford, awaiting another session with Maureen. The clearing of my dad's name and the timing of it buoyed me. Things were not all bad, I told Maureen. I was young, a student at one of the top universities in the world and my dad wasn't going to prison.

'I've been really stressed about the dinner and dreading the speech, but I'm going to be positive. I should be positive,' I said.

'Why does the dinner feel important?'

'They say university is meant to be the best time of your life and I've been miserable for so much of it. Now that my dad has been cleared, the dinner is a chance for me to look at how full the glass really is rather than always complaining that it's almost empty. But I just don't know if I can do that.'

'I see a lot of people here, Mohsin. I'm sure you can,' she said.

After the main course, I had to give the dreaded speech. To distract my audience, I'd bought them one hundred and fifty Kinder Surprise eggs to share, which came with a toy that had to be assembled. They harked back to our childhoods and seemed a great way to divert attention from the speech giver. Watching the childlike smiles on student faces as they compared toys made me sure it was the right decision. I had made a place for myself in this world and it had opened its arms to me. It might not have been the whole of me but it wasn't inauthentic either. Staring round the room, I felt grateful, perhaps for the first time, to be me.

I returned briefly to my room to drop off my camera before going to the after-party. On the way out I paused at the door. I went back inside and turned the camera on to video function and recorded a message to my future self, reminding him that it wasn't all bad. It was intentionally optimistic, forcefully so, and the words were just as much for the present me as they were for the elder. As I hit stop, my phone rang. It was Mum.

'Hi, Ami.'

'Hi, Mochie, sorry to call now, I know it was your dinner tonight.' Her voice was husky.

'No, that's OK. Are you all right?'

'It's your grandmother ... she's in hospital in Lahore. She had a stroke and is in intensive care. The doctors don't think she'll make it through the night.'

'Oh my God,' was all I could muster. I felt like I was being taunted, punished for letting my guard down, for letting myself believe that things could be OK. My grandmother's stroke seemed to make it clear that they could not.

I woke mid-morning the following day to several missed calls from my mum and Abbass. I called back.

'She made it through. She's awake again. The doctors think she'll make a full recovery,' Mum said with a mixture of excitement and relief.

'That's fantastic.'

*

By our next counselling session, the light in me had dimmed to a melancholic hue.

'My grandad was a barrister in Pakistan. Apparently he had four wives. It's weird how some people think it's OK for him to have four wives but I can't have one husband. Not that I want a husband ... I'm just so tired of it.'

'Of what?' Maureen asked.

'Everything. I don't know if I can see this through.'

Maureen said nothing, only held me with her gaze.

I was silent for a long time.

'How do you feel about your grandmother?'

'My dad has been through so much recently. He didn't need this. None of us did. I feel selfish for thinking this way but it's as though I'm being punished. Whenever I think things are working out, something happens in my family to remind me I don't have a right to be happy.'

'You mentioned last time that you were going to try and make yourself go on a date.'

'Well, it wasn't really a date, but I saw that guy in London.' My version of penance was to confess my misdeeds to Maureen, it seemed.

'The film director? How did it go?' We had met in a bar in London weeks earlier. He had walked up to me and told me how handsome I was. No one had ever told me that before, not the way he had. He asked me for my phone number and I almost threw it at him.

'He was flying back from Cannes quite late so he suggested meeting at his place. I ... I didn't want to,' I said.

'Yes, you did,' Maureen said. 'And, that's OK.'

'I'm still two people though! I have these mad sexual urges and my brain just mutes the guilt and lets my dick take over ... it felt seedy. He wanted to go straight to bed and I was completely sober. I hadn't actually been in a bed with a guy before but I couldn't tell him that … I … I sort of froze when he came towards me. I couldn't even look at him. I just lay there, almost dead inside. But then he touched me and I felt a burst of raw energy … like … I can't explain it really. It was like nothing I've ever felt before.'

'It felt good,' she said.

'It was like I wasn't myself. My body knew what to do, as if it had always known and was just waiting to show me. How is that possible? It wasn't anything like I imagined, nothing like it looks on TV. There were moments where I felt like I was floating. But as soon as it was over the bubble burst. I felt as if I had just witnessed something dirty, like these disgusting acts were committed by somebody else. I used to believe sex before marriage was a sin. Perhaps I still do.'

'You feel guilty?'

'Yes. Guilty and repulsed.'

'You won't always feel that way,' she said. 'This was your first proper sexual encounter. It's normal to have a mixture of feelings at this point, gay or straight.'

'He tried to hug me afterwards and I wouldn't let him. My brain was buzzing, and the thought of hugging him made me feel sick.'

'Why the hugging in particular?'

'It just felt too intimate, more intimate than anything else. I felt like God was judging me. And then I imagined my parents seeing me in that state. I went to the bathroom and washed because I felt so disgusting. Then I grabbed my jacket and left.'

'What do you mean? Wasn't it the middle of the night?' I liked how Maureen's question showed a concern for my safety.

'Yes. I wandered around a part of London I didn't recognise. I had to pay a taxi driver to take me to Marble Arch and from there I got the Oxford bus.' On the bus back, I'd felt the relief of escaping the claws of a monster. But wasn't I just trying to run away from something within?

'Mohsin, I think that you see your gay self as contaminating your real self, as if it's somehow toxic, infectious,' Maureen observed. 'When in fact he is an important, valid part of you. You hate him because of what he stands for.'

'Because he stands for everything I'm not. If I accept him I have to re-evaluate everything. Religion, family, job –'

'Why job?'

'Well, why do I study? Because I want to get a good job to support my family and to marry well, but I'm not going to have a family and I don't want a wife, so what exactly am I working hard for?' I paused, then added, 'I think some people are starting to figure out that I'm gay. The student paper has this gossip column and they made this joke about me. I kissed a girl at a party and the writer said he was surprised.'

Even through her silences, Maureen encouraged me to walk the corridors of my mind.

'Does it worry you that people might know?' she asked.

'I used to think there were two types of people in the world – those who could potentially kill themselves and those who couldn't. Now I know life is more complicated than that.'

'Are you saying you're suicidal?'

Suicide felt to me like it might be an atonement. 'I have been. It comes and goes. The other day I considered taking a bunch of sleeping pills. The idea of falling asleep and not waking up was so appealing. The problem is suicide is against Islam too.'

'Do you think your parents would rather a gay son or a dead son?'

I hadn't thought about it that way before. Maureen worked with my feelings like they were the colours of a Rubik's cube she was able to align. My mum was my gateway into the world. I came from her. That's what made it so hard to imagine that she might not want me in it.

'I honestly don't know the answer.' A dead son they could explain. It would be a moment in time and then they might move forward. They'd live with the shame of a gay son for as long as I was alive. I sighed. 'I just feel like I'm going to be depressed forever.'

'You're not depressed, Mohsin,' she said. I looked up at her. 'You're sad and lost and scared and you have every right to be.' Hearing those words gave me hope. 'I want you to do something for me. Let's imagine a future in which you have a son, OK?'

'OK ...' I said.

'Now imagine your son in exactly the situation you are in now– the same history, the same conflicts, the same desires and the same fears. What do you do?'

I had to step back, out of myself to answer her question. I imagined a little boy that had my eyes and my inability to sit still.

'I grab him. I hold him tightly and tell him that he's OK. That he is loved and that I don't give a fuck about religion. That any God who loves me must love him as much.'

'Now think about his sadness. What does *that* make you feel?'

'It makes me angry ... really, *really* angry.'

Digging deep into this pit of anger, I felt something shift inside me. My sense of justice kicked in. The anger felt good, powerful. Like rocket fuel. I wouldn't be stalled by the obstacles put in my path. I would knock them down. I was surer now than ever before that I would not marry a woman. I would live my life as a gay man and, one way or another, there would come a time when I would face my family and force them to face the truth.

24

As I sped through the Eurotunnel, en route to Amsterdam to start the third year of my four-year course, I felt myself undergoing a transformation. I was twenty, no longer a teenager, and in Holland, there would be no more lies. I was gay, and if I couldn't change that, then *I* had to change. A year away was the perfect opportunity.

Brandon was a gregarious gay Canadian master's student also studying at the university. I envied the comfort with which he lived in his skin. His charisma fed off his sexuality rather than thriving in spite of it. His humour made it easy to be friends and I soon became, as he called it, his 'protogay'.

I confided in him, telling him that sometimes I felt possessed by the devil. As his eyes grew wide in disbelief, he said, 'You should never feel that way. Hell, it's 2005 – no one should! Mohsin, look, just look.' He guided me towards the mirror that hung behind the door of my small dorm room in Leiden, an ancient university town just outside Amsterdam. I strained to find something in the reflection that looked attractive to me. I'd divorced my mind from my body, the latter seeming to me to be an agent of perversion, the brownness like a tarnish.

'Mohsin, you're smart, sexy and funny. You have to work with what you've got, and lucky for you, you got a lot! The boys are gonna eat you alive tonight. I'm gonna be batting them away like this!' he said, swinging an imaginary bat.

*

In the bustle of the Amsterdam bar, I lost Brandon for a moment. An older man grabbed me by the hand and led me up a staircase. When we reached the top I saw an open doorway and asked where we were going but he didn't turn round or answer.

'OH NO YOU DON'T!' Brandon grabbed my free hand and yanked. 'Go on in there yourself, you skank! But this one isn't going with you!' he shouted as the man disappeared into the room.

'What's in there?'

'Look, obviously I can't tell you what to do but you need to know that those dark rooms are naaaaasty.'

'What happens?'

'Guys go in there to have SEX!' he screeched. 'And you can catch all sorts of nastiness. No protogay of mine is going in there. If you wanna do that sort of thing, you're gonna have to find yourself a new big sister.'

'You're the only big sister I need, Brandon,' I said, smiling.

'Come on, honey, let's dance.'

Whereas most people told me that my parents had no choice but to accept me for who I was, Brandon respected the complexities but encouraged me not to dwell on them and to focus on more important things. Like boys.

'OK, Mohssy, now this is a game just like any other. The boys love a good chase. You can't seem too keen.'

'If you like someone, why pretend that you don't?' I asked.

'Because men are fickle little bitches. They want what they can't have. So you tell them they can't have it.' He pointed at my bum. 'They want it, they gotta come get it,' he said, hands in the air, moving his torso like a belly dancer. 'Oh and she is your best friend,' he said, pointing to the drink in my hand.

'Brandon – look at them. They just got married!' I said, pointing at the two Dutch men in tuxedos. A small wedding party had come into the bar to celebrate.

'Honey, this was the first country on earth to allow gay marriage. We have a lot to thank them for. Soon other countries will do it too, I'm sure,' he said.

'I'm not.'

'I'd love it though. Wouldn't you?' he asked, watching the couple.

'So when you get married, who'll wear the white dress?'

'Um ... both of us!' he said, twirling on the spot.

Watching the married couple dance with their small group of friends was phenomenal and unlike anything I could imagine for myself. I envied their easy intimacy, the way they looked at each other, beaming with an honest happiness. In the centre of the group I noticed four older people.

'Look, they're dancing with their *parents*!' I shouted with disbelief. I was sure now that it was the most magical thing I'd ever seen.

'Where are you from?' asked the young English guy.

'I'm from London but I'm studying in Leiden,' I said. 'Are you visiting Amsterdam?'

'Yeah ... yeah I am,' he said dismissively. 'I mean, where are you *really* from?'

'Oh, well, I was born in London but –'

'Yeah I gathered that ...'

'My parents are from Pakistan,' I said.

'Pakistan? Really? You don't look it,' he said, laughing in surprise. 'I thought it might be like Spanish or Brazilian or something.'

'What he meant was that I didn't look like a taxi driver or a shop-keeper,' I told Brandon later.

'Fuck that ignoramus,' Brandon said. But I couldn't ignore it, it was a reaction I was all too familiar with. When I looked exotic I was attractive, but once they found out I was Pakistani, they wouldn't want to know. I began lying. Iranian was my fallback choice. It didn't come with the same connotations as Pakistani seemed to. I disappointed myself each time I told the lie but I was sure that my Pakistaniness was a barrier to meeting someone.

'I really hate being gay, Brandon. I know I shouldn't say it but that's how I feel,' I told him over the beats of Sean Paul's 'Temperature'. 'Sometimes I just wish there was some button I could press to make myself straight.'

'Mohssy ... no! I understand why you feel like that but come on. You're lucky to be alive! Think of our gay ancestors in this very city. Nazis everywhere. They had to hide out and not all of them made it, in fact thousands didn't.'

'What do you mean?'

'You don't know about pink triangle?'

'No.'

'Of course you don't! The world conveniently forgets what Hitler did to us so they can keep on discriminating against us without being tarnished by the same Nazi brush.'

'Hitler killed gays?'

'And lesbians and trans people too. The Nazis had internment camps for them just the same as the Jews and made them wear pink triangles. That's why the pink triangle is an LGBT symbol. Get this – if they were Jewish *and* gay they had to wear both the yellow star and the triangle.

There's a monument down the road commemorating it. You have to go and pay your respects.'

Weeks later I sat by the canal, on the pink steps that led to the marble triangle on the water. After my talk with Brandon, I'd researched the treatment of the LGBT community during the war. I had studied World War II practically every year of primary and secondary school and not once in that time had anyone told me that gays had been damned by the Nazis. Perhaps if more people knew that this was a fundamental part of the Nazi ethos, they'd think twice about their own homophobia. This felt like my history too. I imagined growing up in a family that could have shared it with me. Instead I heard it for the first time in a foreign country from a foreign man who was part of my new family, sharing my history with me.

The distance between me and my real family was both geographical and emotional. When my dad called and asked if I'd prayed I lied and thought nothing of it. I was now able to suspend my concern for them almost entirely and think instead about myself. That was until they visited. My mum came with seven-year-old Raza. Before they arrived, my friends helped me 'de-gay' my room, which meant removing any hint of my sexuality. After one friend removed a pink highlighter pen, I knew we'd done a thorough job. My mum cooked a huge meal for the Americans, South Africans, Italians and many others; twenty students in total. During the feast she told everyone about how, earlier that day, I'd taken her to a store where customers could make their own jewellery and how I'd helped her put together the bracelet she now wore. I could feel a collective question in the air: how was it possible that she had no idea that her son might be gay? I got through the visit by hitting pause on the person I was becoming. I de-gayed my mind the way I had my room.

Abbass's visit was not so uneventful. He had always been my fat little brother but he was now a slim, tall, confident young man. On a night out in Leiden, the club played Panjabi MC's 'Mundian To Bach Ke' and he jumped to his feet.

'Remember this?! We danced to it so much in Pakistan.' He grabbed my arm and I rose, reluctantly. I didn't feel entitled to enjoy it anymore, like I'd had my Pakistani card revoked after coming out. Not Abbass though. He bounced straight into the middle of the dance floor and began his repertoire of outlandish and impressive bhangra moves, reminding me instantly of Uncle Tier. Up and down and round and round he went. I swayed side to side, trying to disguise my embarrassment. As he danced, the confidence spilled out of him. We were so different. I could tell that Abbass was strong and comfortable in his skin and he could tell that I was not.

'It's just ridiculous,' I said to him as we cycled along one of the Leiden canals on the last day of his visit. Bright sunshine glistened on the still waters. 'Not only do they expect us to marry a Muslim but a Pakistani Muslim, and not just a Pakistani Muslim but a Pakistani Shia Muslim, and not only a Pakistani Shia Muslim but an educated Pakistani Shia Muslim! That probably only leaves about five people and three of them will be our first cousins! It's impossible. Doesn't it stress you out?'

'Not really,' he replied. 'I've always known that's what they want, but it's what I want too. What about you?'

I veered to avoid a bollard and his question.

'Mohsin, tell me ... are you gay?'

I was stunned. I felt like I was losing control of my bike. That I might swerve straight into the canal. I hoped it would swallow me whole.

I didn't challenge the question. I paused for a moment before I said, 'No.'

As he climbed the steps to board his plane, he sent me a text message telling me he loved me, and that no matter what, he would always be there for me. I was too overwhelmed to speak to anyone. Spending time with him reminded me of how much pain I'd put myself through and how lonely I'd felt. I struggled to calm my frantically pounding heart. I had spent a year in Holland outrunning my old life but it was catching up with me once more.

25

I'd returned from Holland and was about to start my final year at Oxford. I had accepted a job with Linklaters, which I would take up after I had graduated and finished post-degree legal exams. Linklaters was one of the biggest law firms in the world and part of the 'magic circle', the elite group of firms. It was the first-choice destination for top graduates looking for sparkling legal careers in the City but not for me.

Barristers, not solicitors, were the ones who went to court in wigs and gowns. They were the ones I'd seen on TV making grand speeches in dramatic language to juries who hung on their every word. That was who I wanted to be, but barristers were self-employed which came with huge risks; course fees were high and places were extremely competitive. Depending on where you ended up, it could take years to earn more than a teacher's salary. By contrast, my starting salary at Linklaters was more than my parents' combined income. I simply couldn't afford to say no.

It was a Thursday evening in September 2006, a week and a half before I was to return to university. My mum and dad sat me down for a family chat. Abbass was in Thailand so the subject was specifically my future. Nowadays my parents wanted to have these talks frequently to identify the next step in the master plan. In fact they were less about planning and more about enjoying the new reality that presented itself. It was like buying a new pair of shoes for a special occasion. Even though it wasn't time to wear them, you'd remove the box from under the bed and lift the lid, just to take a peek. That's what my parents would do with my future.

Our sitting room had two sofas. They were on one and I sat opposite them on the other. A mixture of excitement and hope emanated from them. I felt older than them in that moment. Coming out had aged me. I felt like I knew more about the world than my parents and this gave me a wisdom they could not share.

The plan, as they saw it, was for me to finish university and then move back home. After my legal exams I would begin a career as a solicitor and eventually consider marriage. Although they were in no particular rush to marry me off, my parents wanted me to start thinking about options and by 'options' they meant suitable brides. The girls had a choice of course. Arranged did not mean forced but that didn't stop the girls from being treated like job applicants, their own desires and expectations condensed into photographs for me to sift through and shortlist.

By this time Mariam, Uncle Makki's daughter, was no longer an option, but three or four families had already enquired if I might be open to the idea of meeting their daughters. My parents spoke of me spending a couple of years at Linklaters, commuting from home of course, and then finding a suitable wife. My culture had the beauty of an ornate birdcage. Rustic and delicate but ultimately criss-crossed with bars designed to prevent the bird from flying away. So many times before I'd nodded and agreed with their vision of the future. It was easy to do when I had no plausible alternative vision of my life. My mum and dad must have imagined my wedding as the jewel in the crown of their Oxford-graduating lawyer son. I had no choice but to stop them in their tracks.

'The thing is, I think I'll probably move in with friends after finals,' I said. I had been reluctant, perhaps scared, of telling them this. And I was right to be.

The idea behind moving out after university was a simple one. I would postpone talk of marriage for as long as possible, blaming my career. I had two younger brothers who, for reasons of tradition, would be unable to marry before I did, but there were more pressing concerns. Moving out would give me the freedom and the privacy I had become used to at university and now longed for again. It would also protect them from the truth, at least for a few years. Put simply, I was running away.

I couldn't imagine living with the daily weight of expectation that came from being at home. So I would do what any sensible person would in that situation. I would leave. I knew this would not be easy on my parents, but in my head, it didn't mean I was rejecting their plans for me, just delaying them. I was leaving on the understanding that I would eventually return home and marry. Long term this was not a viable solution but I wasn't ready to tell the truth and not sure I ever would be. Deceit felt like the least worst option.

My dad was upset but believed me when I told him nothing had changed. My mum, however, was not fooled. Although she could not have known why, she sensed instantly that things between us were now different. I'd gone to Oxford and made white friends. I'd had middle-class experiences. Our cultural contract was inconsistent with the life that I appeared to have chosen for myself.

When it became clear to my mum that I really was going to leave, she froze. She made me feel as if she was looking at me for the first time. I was a stranger to her and an unwelcome one. Baby carriers provide the option of placing the infant so that he or she faces the parent or looks out, facing the world. I imagined that most parents would choose to let their child see the world, whereas mine preferred I see only them.

'If you leave, that's it. You won't come back. You know that,' she said with a desperation no child should hear in a parent's quivering voice. With my words, I had set their plans alight and they were both transfixed by the blaze.

I tried to speak, but on my mum's cue my dad asked me to leave them to talk. The worst thing was that he asked politely, in a tone I'd heard him use when talking to English people.

'We must respect your decision,' he said. 'But we need time to think.' Think about what?

Apparently, parents of gay children often guess this is the case before they are told. Did they know? Had they discussed how worried they were about their eldest son? Had they resolved that they loved him anyway and that he would remain a member of their family because he was their child, their responsibility? Maybe I wouldn't need to leave.

I tried to speak again.

'Just leave,' my mum said. I didn't recognise the disappointment in her voice at first. As the golden child, I'd never heard it before, and it marked the distance between us. They didn't know anything about me.

The next morning I woke up to an empty house. I spent most of the day preparing for the start of the final year and was upstairs when I heard my mum come in from work. Her back was to me when I walked into the kitchen. Although she acknowledged my presence, the next few minutes passed as if I were invisible. I tried to make conversation, but it was clear she was still upset so I tried to address the subject directly. She didn't want to talk about it and certainly not to me. I gave her the space she needed from the stranger who had arrived the night before. The next day, a Saturday, was the same. My dad told me to give her time. Without saying so, he made it clear that, although she would be OK, I was responsible for hurting her. Their reactions felt unreasonable but I knew that they were not. They were loving people who had tried their best to give me a life they couldn't have. Yes, their dreams were different from mine but they were still dearly held dreams.

I had told myself I was doing the right thing. Perhaps misguidedly, I thought I was protecting them from the shame and the loss that would inevitably follow if I stayed.

By Sunday my resolve had unravelled. Was it a greater evil to let them believe I no longer respected our cultural values or was the greater evil the truth? I resented being blamed for the breakdown. They would be hurt and it was because of me but that wasn't the same as it being my fault. Feeling damned for the way you are born is hard enough. Having to protect those you love from the truth is harder still. But being vilified in order to protect them, that was a guilt I could not bear. What was the point of this facade, if they'd be heartbroken either way?

My heart felt parched from the absence of their affection and support at a time when I was in severe need of it. I couldn't think clearly. Or perhaps in that moment, although I didn't know it, I had the clarity of thought that comes only after years of lies.

Late that afternoon I approached my mum's bedroom door. I had no agenda. I had spent years trying to hold the different parts of myself together. The circular thinking had been exhausting. I just wanted to be loved.

She was sitting on the bed when I entered. Silence. I struggled to find anything to say. I was immediately overcome with grief. It rushed out, without any forewarning. A dam of water cracking open. When I opened my mouth all I could manage was the heaving noise you make before you start crying. I had let my guard down and needed to get out of there. She couldn't see me cry, especially not like this, otherwise she'd know something was wrong. I turned to leave. I didn't make eye contact but her motherly concern shone brightly in my peripheral vision as she rose to follow me. I ran into my bedroom and closed the door, by now crying uncontrollably. I don't think one can fully appreciate what it means to cry uncontrollably until it happens to you. It isn't your eyes that shed tears. It isn't your mouth that groans. It is your soul weeping.

There was no lock on the door so I sat against it to prevent her from coming in. I covered my mouth to stifle the sobs, sobs which were filled with anger, guilt, despair and a deep, piercing sorrow.

She forced her way in with little difficulty. If I had had any energy to fight, I would have kept the door closed, to protect her from the harm that my secret would inflict. Instead I held my head in my arms as if to protect myself from a physical attack. I tried to say 'I'm sorry' but could only rock back and forth.

My mum was on the floor with her arms wrapped around me. She asked me what was wrong.

'Are you in trouble? Have you done something you shouldn't?' I shook my head. 'Are you sick?' I had once considered telling them I had cancer. They'd be so relieved I wasn't dying that they might accept me. 'Were you abused?' I just shook my head and continued to cry.

I couldn't say *I am gay*; those three words were too coarse, they wouldn't be enough. I wanted to tell her that I'd known from a very young age, that I'd vowed to keep it a secret, that I had promised myself I would never act upon it. I wanted to say that I had turned to God for help, prayed for a cure five times a day, that on pilgrimage, when she told me God would give me whatever I asked for, she had been wrong and I was still waiting. How could I tell her that I had reached the point where I no longer cared whether I lived or died? That I had started drinking because it was easier than always feeling dirty. That as a teenager I had considered an exorcism. That I was ashamed of myself. That it wasn't a choice. And that I was sorry.

So I said nothing.

'What is it, Mochie?'

Mochie, my childhood nickname. She could see now how helpless I really was.

Eventually she asked, 'Are you gay?'

I saw my mum holding on to the vision of her life as if she were clutching a snow globe, within which lived her whole world, her husband, three sons, their wives, their children, her grandchildren. And then I saw myself grabbing the snowy landscape from her hands and throwing it to the ground.

The only word clearly articulated from my mouth as I sobbed was 'Yes!'

26

My mum was not the first person in my family I had come out to. After Abbass's visit to Holland, his actions, rather than any words exchanged between us, made three things abundantly clear. He knew, he was supportive and he wouldn't tell Mum and Dad. Earlier the same year we were both at home from university.

'Did you get my text message?' he asked.

'Which … one?' I said. My words tried to hide what my face could not.

'You know which one, Mohsin. You didn't reply. I mean, it's OK,' he rushed to add. 'I wasn't expecting a reply but I just wanted to make sure you got it.'

He sat on my bed in my room, at the very edge, as if he was ready to take flight. He looked at me and looked away again. Opened his mouth to speak but said nothing. It was time.

'I did get the message and there is something I need to tell you,' I said.

'So I was right?'

In that moment, things seemed to slow down. A million thoughts rushed through my head, the most prominent that everything before now had been leading me begrudgingly to this point.

'Yes, you're right,' I said. And then it was finally done. The word 'gay' wasn't used by either of us. It seemed too explicit, too raw.

His face wrinkled like a scrunched-up piece of paper as he began to cry. I hesitated at first, fearing he might not want my dirty gay hands anywhere near him. Although emotion stirred inside me, his distress acted as a catalyst, kicking me into big brother mode. I put my arm around him and told him it was OK. Instinctively I could tell that the essence of his sadness came from our bond, not the one between him and his faith.

'I'm just, I'm just so sorry for those horrible things I said ... I'm sorry you had to go through it alone.' With those few words he told me he understood the extent of my isolation, felt it even. It was the one response I hadn't anticipated. In a film this would have been the point where I cried and we hugged. But my heart was elsewhere, hiding from the reaction I thought I would get, not the one that I did. I responded by thanking him, too stunned to know what else to say. A part of me had once wished for a different family and that part was now ashamed for having underestimated my brother.

'Just promise me one thing,' he said. My insides shrivelled. Was he about to ask me to abstain?

'Promise me this isn't a choice. That you aren't doing this to the family because you want to.' It was as if he had risen above us and was looking down at the scene from a bird's-eye view. I loved him more in that moment than ever before. He got it straight away. Did I choose for my heart to beat or my lungs to demand air? And he was right. This was not just happening to me. It was happening to us.

'I promise,' I said.

'Mum and Dad can never know,' he said, wiping his eyes.

'We don't have to talk about that now. Don't worry, I'm not telling them any time soon.'

'One more thing.' I nodded and braced myself for an uncomfortable question. 'Have you tried KFC?'

'What?' I was startled.

'Come on, have you? You told me when I visited that you weren't really practising. Mohsin, tell me, is it as tasty as it looks?' Growing up, a family friend owned numerous KFCs but we weren't allowed to try the food because it wasn't halal. The torture of having to say no, not just to fried chicken but to the original KFC, had clearly haunted Abbass.

'Yes, I have tried it and it's fucking delicious.' I smirked, wondering whether I might be dreaming.

After I told my mum, she deflated, her five-foot-ten frame shrinking before my eyes. I knew that her reaction would haunt me until the day I died or, if the moment ever arrived, until she truly forgave me for what I had done to her. She didn't go to work for the next two days. On the third day she left for the school but came home an hour later because she was so upset. Layla had got up at the crack of dawn that morning and taken the Oxford bus to London to see me. She had only been in the house twenty minutes before I had to ask her to leave – I wasn't sure my mum was ready to face the idea that this wasn't a complete secret. Mum took the rest of the week off, at first retreating to bed, but then emerging with new determination.

'I am going to save you from this. I will find a way. I'm not going to lose you,' she told me. My mum was a fighter. Maybe I had been too defeatist, too readily accepting of my sexuality.

My dad asked me if everything was OK with Mum and I said I hadn't noticed anything, but it was like ignoring a large bull ransacking the room we were standing in.

'I'm going to take Mohsin to Mecca,' I overheard her telling my dad in the living room. In a panic, I thought they might remove me from London and force me into a marriage. But that was absurd. My parents were not like that.

I feared the situation would put a strain on my mum's heart, that it might stop beating suddenly from the stress I had put her through. In that moment, I was willing to do anything to make her pain stop. I considered texting Abbass in Thailand but he could do nothing from so far away except worry.

The situation was spiralling out of my control and I didn't know what to do. I needed a grown-up but it couldn't be Uncle Tier because my mum had forbidden it. My dad wasn't even an option. I'd suggested telling him the very same day. The mad love I knew he had for me meant there was a chance, albeit a very small one, that he might just be able to cope. The fear in my mum's face at the mere thought of it was enough to deter me.

I wrote to Maureen who pointed out that my mum was at the very beginning of an emotional process I had already been through. She would need time. Meanwhile, I needed to stand my hard-won ground. She also said that what I had done was courageous. This took me by surprise. Reckless, certainly. Idiotic, definitely. But courageous? Courage suggested bravery, when all I felt was fear, I was drowning in it. We agreed to meet when I returned to Oxford for my final year.

Abbass wasn't expecting me to collect him from the airport, but he had to know. As I waited, the world felt oppressively real. I watched people scurrying to catch flights and longed to be one of them; to get on a plane and never come back.

'What are you doing here?' he asked.

'Erm ... well ...'

'You told her, didn't you? Is she ok?'

'Not really.'

'Are you ok?'

'Not really.' He gave me a hug.

'But you can't tell Dad, he'll kill you.' I wasn't sure if he was speaking figuratively or literally, but was too scared to ask him to clarify. I began to doubt my earlier optimistic feelings about my dad. They seemed flimsy and unconvincing now. Was the loving father I knew really capable of hurting me?

I was going back to Oxford and Mum and I stood in the rainy car park of our mosque about to say goodbye. The rules between us hadn't just changed, they'd been blown away in a gust. There were traditions for every eventuality in our culture. How we should speak to elders, how food should be served to guests, how a child should demonstrate respect for his parents. There were no traditions for how a mother and her son should interact after he had told her he was gay. We had to find a way to simply be, but were scrambling in the dark. She sobbed as we hugged.

My earliest memory was of my first day at nursery. It had large windows that looked onto the playground. My mum had waited patiently for me to stop crying but I would not let her or Abbass go. Eventually she was advised to leave, that their presence was making it more difficult for me to acclimatise. I saw her reluctantly push the pram away, Abbass leaning over the side, watching his big brother getting smaller and smaller. I felt like that boy again, losing his mother. Being left by her in an unfamiliar world, for there was no place for me in hers any more.

My mum hid her emotions as effectively as a toddler. It was clear to her brothers that something was wrong when she turned up in Northampton with puffy red eyes and monosyllables for conversation.

'She's been crying all the way up the motorway and now she won't tell us what's wrong,' Uncle Zain said to me during one of the many phone calls he made. Despite their concerns my mum refused to explain, saying only that this was the worst time in her life and she didn't want to talk about it. She was embarrassed and afraid, emotions I had felt myself when I first came out. But her loving brothers refused to let up.

'Is she sick?' Zain asked. 'Tier thinks it might be cancer and she's trying to protect us. If she's sick you have to tell us so we can try and help her.'

'She's not sick,' I said, resisting the urge to add that they might, however, think I was.

On more than one occasion my tutor called me into his room to discuss my underperformance. 'You have the chance to get a great education here, Mohsin. Don't waste this opportunity,' he pleaded with me. I listened respectfully before telling him, as I had several times before, that I understood what he was saying and that I would try harder. But a few days into my final year I walked out of another mock exam, barely finishing writing my name before doing so. I'd done zero preparation. All the will that studying required had been expended on trying to keep myself and my mum from falling apart. This was a problem because in a few months, through nine three-hour exams over ten days, I'd be tested on everything I was supposed to have learned in the previous four years. The glitch was that I'd learned next to nothing and had no choice but to do an entire Oxford law degree in nine months.

Another call from Uncle Zain came as I crossed the vast empty quad to return to my room.

'Listen, I'm sorry but I can't tell you. It has to be her,' I said quickly, to pre-empt him asking me again. This truth was not mine to tell. It was about me but it didn't concern me. It was a truth between her and her brothers.

'It's all right, Fag Bag! Well, actually I guess I'd better not call you that any more, eh?' He laughed nervously.

'So she told you?'

'Look, I think your mum is mad. She seems to believe God is punishing her for not being a good enough Muslim. Now you know me, I'm not that religious, but I told her, I said God doesn't work that way! She should just love you. You're not a drug dealer or a murderer. You're a good boy. This isn't about her, it's about you. But I do agree that you can't tell your dad.'

'Thanks, Uncle Zain,' I replied. I didn't know what else to say. My energy was almost depleted. It felt like a fight just to get out of bed these days.

Later the same day, Uncle Tier called. It was the fourth time he'd tried to reach me and the first time I had decided to answer. Disappointing him was a feeling I could not bear.

'I'm just relieved, you know,' he said.

'Relieved?'

'I was really worried about her health. I've told her that it's OK to be upset but ultimately you're her son and she has to support you. Can I come and see you this weekend?'

When Uncle Tier came to Oxford with his wife, leaving their two young children with my nan back in Northampton, he became more than just the uncle I'd known as a child. He became a three-dimensional person to me, a friend capable of giving me unconditional support. His designer stubble was complemented by his style, a style I wasn't sure I'd ever noticed before. He wore a brown wool blazer with a pocket square to match a navy shirt underneath. A flat cap sat high on his head offsetting his square-framed glasses. He was a schools finance manager and popular with his colleagues. We couldn't take two steps through their local town centre without someone noticing his tall stature and pausing to say hello.

We sat in a coffee shop. Uncle Tier and his wife had offered to meet me in college but I had intentionally picked somewhere I wouldn't be able to get emotional. Immediately after we ordered, he cut to the chase. He took off his hat, revealing the last remnants of hair on his head. He told me he loved me, that there was nothing wrong with me. I wanted to hug him, to cry and to tell him I was sorry, so deeply sorry. But I did none of those things. I was unemotional, I had to be. I had learned to weather these storms by becoming the anchor and the anchor could not afford to sway, otherwise the ship, and everyone on it, couldn't steady. Inside though, my smile stretched as wide as an ocean.

Layla suggested I set up a website called AsianGayShamMarriage.com 'and find a lesbian to marry'. She joked but those things really happened and I did consider it. Some friends thought they were being supportive by criticising my mum's reaction, telling me to think of myself and not of her. This advice, however well intentioned, was misguided. It assumed I lived in their world and not in hers. In fact I felt, now more than ever before, that I lived in neither. How lonely it was to take on an entire culture and faith by myself. But I wasn't alone because I had Maureen. My sessions with her proved a pit stop for my racing mind.

'Do you think your mother's reaction is fair?' she asked.

'I once had an argument with my dad about how their expectations were unfair. Do you know what he said? "What makes you think I have to be fair?" And he was right.'

'You don't think fairness, or a sense of justice, applies to families?'

'Maybe.'

'Would you hope to treat your children fairly?'

'Yes.'

'Why?'

'Because ... because it's the right thing to do.'

'Then what makes your parents' behaviour any different?' Maureen made me want more for myself, it was her superpower. But at the same time I was frustrated by her challenges to my assumptions. She didn't seem to understand what was best for me and my family. But gradually it became clear that she understood it all too well as the objective observer. My own understanding was clouded because I was in too deep. She began showing me that what was best for me wasn't the same thing as what was best for them.

After coming out to my mum, I spent most of my free time shuttling back and forth between London and Oxford. When I was at home, I longed to be back at the university, away from the turmoil I had created. But back in Oxford, I thought only of being close to Mum, as if by being there I could help absorb the emotional impact.

When I returned home for Christmas my dad surreptitiously mentioned that he needed to speak to me when my mum wasn't around. My stomach lurched. He knew.

'There is something I have to talk to you about, Mohsin,' he said calmly, the two of us sitting at the kitchen table. 'It's about the recent events with your mother.' My heart pounded.

'Dad, I ... I was going to tell you ...'

'Oh, so you know?'

'Know?'

'That's she's going through the menopause?'

'Menopause?'

'Yes – well, at least I think so. Her mood has been so up and down lately. I tried asking her about it but I think she doesn't want to talk about it with me which I can understand. It's a complicated process.'

I wanted to laugh and cry but I did neither.

27

Before the onslaught of my finals, I went home one last time. My mum was in an even more sombre mood than usual. She had retreated into herself.

'Mum, what's the matter?' I asked.

'I went on that website you suggested,' she replied. I had found an organisation for gay Muslims.

'OK ...' I said.

'Well, I saw this one photo where they all had their faces disguised, and they were on what looked like a gay rights march in the centre of London. One of them had a blue T-shirt ... and ... well, I checked in your room and you have a blue T-shirt too.' She peered at me as if I were a horror scene about to unfold.

'MUM! I've never been to Pride. That wasn't me,' I said through a sigh of relief that matched her own. But when I retold the story to Maureen, it lost its humour. Maureen reflected that although I was not the boy in the blue T-shirt, it was what I was working towards becoming and fore-warned me that at some point that's who my mum might have to face.

'You might need to be careful about what you promise her, because some promises you might not want to keep. But, in any event, none of this is important at the moment Mohsin, because you have final exams just around the corner.'

'Three, two, one ... GO!' the exam invigilator shouted in a thick Scottish accent from the front of the room, his black scholar's gown bouncing with the exaggerated waving of his arms. The countdown had a way of doubling my heartbeat as each number was called. Day ten, exam nine of nine.

Opening the paper, I caught myself saying 'Bismillah', the prayer that begins every chapter in the Quran, the repetition of which was second nature to me. It means 'in the name of God' but could I ask for God's watchful eye during the most important exams I'd ever take? It was hypocritical. Might I fail if I didn't say it? Was this like finding God on my deathbed? He had abandoned me and I him. I hadn't thought about it and now there was no time. Although I had refrained from saying Bismillah for all my other exams, this was my last chance.

'Bismillah ir-Rahman ir-Rahim,' I whispered to myself, before turning over the page.

On the morning of the last day of university life, I packed the belongings I had accumulated over the previous four years into Maureen's car and she drove me back to London. In the passenger seat of her Volvo estate, I cried.

As the ancient spires disappeared from view, everything I was leaving behind seemed to be calling me back, refusing to let go. I was saying goodbye to the city that had made me who I was right now. I had gone through the magical wardrobe into Narnia. Into a land filled with experiences I'd never known before and couldn't begin to understand when I had first arrived. It was not just a degree, but a key to a privileged world I could now live in. Oxford taught me I was not white but also gave me an education in whiteness. It told me I was raised poor but left me richer. And it made me face the reality that I was gay while giving me the space and freedom of mind to accept it. When I'd arrived four years earlier, it was easier to look down at my shadow than at the road ahead. I was excited about the world, about all the different cities and people and places and things to see and do, but it was an excitement with caveats. For now, I was saying goodbye to Narnia and entering the wardrobe once again, only this time it would lead me back into my parents' house. I had agreed to move back to the home in which the old me had once lived. But the old me was gone.

A month later my tutor called with my results. To my surprise and his, I passed with a decent grade. Although students were allocated a maximum of two tickets for the graduation ceremony some months after results, I managed to secure seven. My mum in an elegant black-and-white shalwar kameez, my dad in a characteristically smart suit and tie, Abbass, Raza, Uncle Tier looking suave, his wife, my nan, both also in traditional Pakistani dress, and me in a gown and graduation cap. The sight of so many of us walking into the ceremonial hall seemed a scene from a sketch show but we revelled in it.

The ceremony was almost entirely in Latin. The expressions on my family's faces reminded me of my own misgivings when I first started at the university. My nan was squinting; she didn't really speak English and must have assumed they were just using more words she had never heard before. Later that day, when Layla and Ish, who had graduated the year before, came up from London to join us for a celebratory dinner I took them to the side for a quick briefing.

'You have to remember – I'm not gay and I don't drink. OK, now let's go ...' I said, shoving them through the restaurant entrance behind my ravenous family.

During the graduation meal with my family and friends, I thought about my old secondary school and how lucky I was to have got this far, with help from so many people. It seemed unfair that most of the kids I went to school with would not have access to the world of opportunities I was about to step into. My thoughts were interrupted by Raza reaching for my water. My family casually took from each other's plates and glasses. Even though I knew it was impossible, I couldn't shake the fear that I might infect them, and Raza in particular, with an STD I could have caught.

Although Uncle Tier and Abbass were supportive, they could not force my mum to think differently or change the way my dad might react. I was at the dinner but my heart had already begun to withdraw from them. I couldn't tell them about God. About how I anguished over whether I believed or not, concluding there needed to be a fourth category added to the 'believer, agnostic, atheist' list. Those labels all required me to pick a side but I didn't want to pick and didn't want to say I was agnostic because I wasn't. The fourth group was for those who simply did not engage with the question. I blocked it out.

Our Christmas tradition was to drive up to Northampton and spend it with my nan and grandad, Zain and Tier and their families. Every year when people asked whether my family celebrated Christmas I said *no* but added the caveat that we did get together, buy each other Christmas presents, place them under the decorated tree and eat a halal roast Turkey.

Uncle Tier and I went for a walk in the park across from his house.

'Your mum feels like you might have outgrown them,' he said.

'Were those the words she used?' I asked. Growing apart I could understand but to suggest that I was somehow better than them upset me. He could see how disheartened I was.

'Look, son, you aren't the only one with a secret,' he said as we sat on a bench opposite a pond whose water was freezing over.

191

'What do you mean?' I said.

'Well ...' He took a deep breath. 'When you were about five years old, I had a son with an Englishwoman.'

'Oh ... wow! I can't believe I never knew. Does Mum know? Does Nan know? That can't have been easy.'

'It wasn't.' He shook his head. 'But yes, they all know, so it isn't a secret, well, it is, but you know what I mean.'

'I'm glad to hear it. How did Nan take it?'

'She was fantastic. I was so upset when I told her and she just took me in her arms and said she loved me. Your mum did too.' I felt a pang of jealousy.

'Why didn't you tell me before?'

'When your mum told me about you and I came down to visit I did consider it but that moment was about you, not me.'

'What does Dad think?' I asked, hoping this would give me some clue as to how he might react to my situation.

'He doesn't know,' Uncle Tier said.

We had too many secrets and I couldn't understand why. The truth was something we conspired to suppress. Choked it almost to death, for fear of what it might do if set free. In actual fact it was us who were being choked by our secrets, not the other way round.

'Even after fifteen years, your mum still isn't sure how he'd react. She thinks he'd disapprove, so we decided never to tell him.' I couldn't help but wish I had the same luxury.

28

From the moment my mum knew the truth about me, I wanted desperately to tell my dad but she and Abbass feared what he might do. My dad was a devout, proud and reserved man. He laughed openly with his sons, his wife and some of his friends, but to the rest of the world, he was a serious Muslim father and husband. Concepts such as respect and honour were fundamental to him. My dad had never hit us. And yet we feared it. Perhaps the fear was not of the physical. Violence can be a destructive force but so can exposing shameful secrets.

I had more exams approaching, legal exams I would have to pass before I could begin working at Linklaters in September 2009. I had decided to sit the New York legal exams too, so that I could be a qualified lawyer in both England and America. The US exams were hard work but success would provide an escape route to a full life in a country a long way away from my family, far enough away that I might never have to tell my dad. I was twenty-three years old and still thinking about running away from home. Linklaters was funding my place at a special law school in London and I was in the school's central London library all the time, spending four days on English law and three days on American law, trying not to confuse the two or tear out my hair.

'Hello?' I said, stepping away from my desk and answering the phone.

'Hi, Mohsin, where are you?' Abbass asked.

'Where do you think? I'm at the bloody library trying to figure out how two countries could have such different laws on murdering someone. I'll tell you one thing, it's making me want to murder someone ...'

'Mohsin, you have to come home right now.'

I arrived home to find Mum sitting on the sofa, her head bowed, unable to face whatever it was that had forced Abbass to summon me. I'd become accustomed to her avoiding my gaze. We were becoming strangers to one another. I was her son in name but any love for me seemed reserved for the dutiful boy she once knew, nothing was left for the man I was becoming.

'The mosque is talking about it ... about you, they ... they know,' said Abbass. I was an adult and yet still dealing with people gossiping like schoolchildren. I was supposed to react as if I was ashamed, I realised. The voices of self-righteousness were trying to force me to engage with the scariest thing I would ever have to do before I was ready. Abbass's voice had a distinct tone to it. He was speaking from a place in his heart in which neither hope nor ambition lived. My mum still did not raise her head, unable to face the shame, to face me.

There was chatter in my local community about the fact that I was attracted to men. The starkness of it was humiliating. I imagined them taking satisfaction in the demise of the mosque's momentary wonder child. Oxford was now meaningless. I told Abbass I needed to think and went upstairs to call Maureen, hoping to God that she would answer. I couldn't let my dad find out from someone else, I told her. The only thing worse than having a gay Muslim son had to be finding out about it from someone at the mosque. She agreed it would be unfair on him to find out from anyone else but also wanted me to know that it was unfair that I was having to do this on someone else's timetable and that it was OK to be scared. I was petrified.

When I went back downstairs, Abbass and my mum told me they did not think we should tell him. I could see the fear on their faces and I knew that *we* did not have to tell him. I had to do it. It was the hardest thing to do but also the right thing to do. I would tell him that evening. They begged me not to, he would need time, I should do it at the weekend instead. It was really my mum who needed time. Abbass was certain that my dad would throw me out. They braced themselves for a breakdown that might change things forever. I was scared but excited too – for the liberation that truth brings is what overcomes fear.

Finally it was agreed: I'd tell my dad in a couple of weeks at Easter weekend. Not because it had any spiritual significance, but because it was followed by a public holiday, giving him time off from the post office, if he needed it. The days leading up to Easter prickled with nervous anticipation. At one point my dad asked us if something was wrong. I wanted to tell him right then but I knew my mum wasn't ready. We would soon be in deep water and she needed a moment to catch her breath before we dived in.

He spoke English perfectly well but my dad's first language was Urdu, as was mine. When Asian parents raised their voices in discipline it was most often in Urdu. English was a tool we had borrowed from the outside world; it was not the language of our home. The idea of saying the words '*I am gay*' out loud sent shivers down my spine. Saying it in Urdu didn't seem like an option. I didn't know a respectful word for homosexual in Urdu – I wasn't sure there was one. To use our shared language to tell my dad seemed like betrayal, but English would formalise things between us, somehow make me gayer. The day before Easter Sunday, I decided instead to write him a letter.

As I began to put the words down, my hand shook. I tried reading it to my mum and Abbass but wasn't able to get through it. Abbass took the sheet of paper from me and read it out loud. I felt so completely exposed I left the room. When I came back he was at the part where I confessed I had cried every day, that I had thought about killing myself but decided that a gay son was better than a dead one. Abbass had tears running down his cheeks. I stood at the door, steadying myself against the frame, trying not to get even more emotional. Reading that letter together was the most support I had ever received from them.

On the morning of Easter Sunday, Abbass and my mum tried once more to dissuade me, but I stood firm: this moment of revelation was already long overdue.

My parents were going to the mosque that evening. I would face my dad when they came home. Uncle Tier agreed to be there because of the unspoken fear Dad might turn violent.

When Mum and Dad left, I took the opportunity to pack some items, in case I was thrown out of the house. I would move in with friends until I started working and then rent somewhere for myself. I had tried to pack the previous day but it had made the whole thing too intimidatingly real.

Abbass walked in and watched me putting clothes and books into a rucksack.

'At least you get the bigger room now,' I said.

Uncle Tier arrived and took me into his arms the instant I opened the door.

'You can do this, son. If you want me to, I will do it for you but I know that you can do it because you are a man now. A strong man. And I will be right next to you.'

I looked out the front room window obsessively. I wanted as much forewarning as possible.

'They should be here by now,' I said to Abbass and Uncle Tier. We'd arranged for Raza to sleep over at a cousin's house. 'Maybe she told him?'

'No way – Mum couldn't do that even if she wanted to.'

And then there it was. A car approaching, two headlights drawing closer and closer, before it stopped and the lights were switched off. It was bad enough that it was a Sunday. I should have told him during the day. Things always seemed worse in the dark. My nerves had become leeches crawling over my skin, sucking dry my resolve. I couldn't use the letter, I had to face it, say it out loud.

I went to the door. Behind me stood Uncle Tier and Abbass. As I greeted my dad, he looked over my shoulder and asked what Tier was doing there. Behind him, my mum had come to the end of the road, no longer able to contain her anguish. She let out a scream, releasing years of obedient silence. If she tried to speak, the words were unintelligible. Abbass took her into the kitchen. My dad, dumbfounded by her behaviour, wanted to follow but I stopped him, gesturing him instead into the living room.

Uncle Tier explained to my dad that I had something to tell him. I asked him to check on my mum. I was shaking and noticeably upset. It was a sight with which my dad was unfamiliar. The strong son he knew had vanished. My mum's cries from the kitchen became the backdrop to what I was about to say.

'Dad ...' I paused to take what felt like it might be my last breath. Ever. 'Dad, there's ... there's something I have to tell you ...' I explained that I had let go of my faith although what I really wanted to say was that it had let go of me. I told him that during our pilgrimages to Syria,

I'd prayed for things to be different. I told him that when I got into Oxford I thanked God but asked that it be taken away. I told him that my 'problem' had led to my falling apart. An American woman who was first my counsellor and now my friend had saved me from doing something stupid. My voice shook as the words tumbled out of me. Finally I looked him in the eyes and said: 'Dad, I'm gay and I didn't choose to be this way.' They were the truest, most honest words my mouth had spoken and yet they were not enough. If only I was able to make him reach into me and feel my debilitating pain. But words were all I had at my disposal. They polluted the air and, I was sure, the rest of my life but, in that moment in the first seconds afterwards, I felt like a person born in captivity that had taken his first breath of free air.

My dad was wearing a scarf around his neck which he hadn't yet had a chance to remove. He pulled it across his face to muffle the groans. Within seconds my mum, Abbass and Uncle Tier were in the room. My mum and dad were both weeping and there was something touching about seeing them holding on to each other. I couldn't recall seeing them behave so tenderly towards one another. My mum was shouting in Punjabi, 'How could I tell you? How could I tell you? I didn't want it to hurt you.' I looked over at Abbass and Uncle Tier for a lifeline but they were frozen, braced for the fallout.

I pulled forward the coffee table and sat on it, facing my parents. I said I was sorry. Their heads remained buried in each other.

After calming my mum down, my dad finally spoke.

'I still love you just the same,' he said. He got up and hugged me.

'Mohsin has his bags packed upstairs, you know,' Uncle Tier said.

'No! No, no. You are not going anywhere. You are my son and I love you. I will support you in any way that I can,' he said, pointing a finger at me. He took my mum's hand and led her up to their room. He needed to speak to her alone. I could not begin to imagine what they might say to each other. It had felt like the longest day of my life and it was over.

I walked into my bedroom. I glanced at the packed bag waiting for me on the floor and the letter I'd scribbled resting on the bed. I'd survived. If I could survive this, I could survive anything. Or so I thought. The following week, a witch doctor arrived at the house.

PART THREE

29

After coming out to my parents, our family chats stopped. For them, there was no longer a future to plan and it was difficult for me not to be affected by this point of view. I imagined each day of my life as the page of a colouring book, each with a unique, intricate and indecipherable pattern. There were a finite number of pages. I wanted the remaining pages to burst with bright blues and reds and yellows instead of the blacks and greys of the ones that went before but after abdicating my role as the eldest son, the palette seemed only to offer more darkness.

My mum and I sat in silence in front of the TV, as she flicked between channels.

'How are you doing?' she said. It was a hollow question that begged a hollow reply.

'I'm fine,' I said.

When I was a child, my mum and I would play a game.

'OK, let me see if I can smell your face without giving you a kiss,' she would say.

'OK, but you always end up kissing me,' I would reply.

'Let's try it and see.' And then she would pull me in close, smell my cheek, put our noses together and suddenly, as if overwhelmed by the scent, smother me in kisses. I remembered that now as I sat beside her, sensing that my presence was like a bad smell.

Although my dad hadn't thrown me out, I was still the pink elephant in the room.

'Mohsin, are you doing anything on Sunday?'

'Just going to the library again, Mum.'

'Your father wants you to be home on Sunday afternoon, OK?'

'Why?' I asked. Neither of us looked at the other.

'We have a guest coming,' she said. As she continued to flick between channels, *Will & Grace* popped into view. I instantly tensed. I knew from Abbass that she couldn't watch it any more, as if all she could see in it now was the gay part of me. Not the son I was, nor the lawyer I was becoming, just a flamboyant man mocking her from the screen. One of the characters was complaining about how hard it was to fall in love as a gay man. I resented how easily this fictitious, attractive lawyer thousands of miles away was able to worry about finding a partner.

I'd wondered whether it would have been easier to tell them the truth with a partner to support me. I imagined texting him in moments such as these, when it was unbearable to be at home, when I guessed something might be happening at the weekend for which I needed his support. Before I could ask her who was coming on Sunday, my mum got up and left the room.

Are you coming home soon? Dad's asking, read the text from Abbass. I packed up my books in the library, now convinced that something strange was going on. As I walked up to our front door, I saw an unfamiliar figure in the front room.

'Mohsin, I'm glad you're home. There is someone here I'd like you to meet.' Abbass peered down at me apologetically from the landing and I knew that he wished he'd told me what was going on but had been warned not to. I resented myself for causing him distress.

In the living room an unassuming Pakistani man in his late fifties was sipping tea on the sofa. His face bore wrinkles resembling worn brown leather.

'Mohsin, this is Dr Saab.' That clearly wasn't his name – *saab* translated as 'sir', used to indicate respect. More to the point, he didn't look like a doctor and, even if he were, I didn't think I needed one.

'Salaam, Dr Saab,' I said.

My dad sat down next to him. In a small act of defiance I remained standing.

'Dr Saab would like to discuss some things with you and I would like you to listen to him very carefully and do what he says.'

'What sort of doctor are you?' I said.

'Can I suggest that Mohsin and I go for a walk? How does that sound to you?' He ignored my question. He spoke with a Pakistani accent, gently, politely, as if to erase the hostility I was giving off.

'OK,' I said.

We walked down the street and, at my suggestion, into the nearby woodland, bathed in spring sunshine. A familiar place that now felt different, vaguely threatening. Among the trees I wondered whether it would have been wiser to stick to the roads, but I knew that my parents would never let any harm come to me and that, in any event, I could probably take this old man.

'Your father has told me what you told him last week' he began, in an attempt to get me to open up. But I would not. Not until I knew what course of treatment this *doctor* proposed and, more importantly, what illness he thought he was curing.

'OK,' I said.

'Would you like to tell me about it?'

'Uncle, why don't you tell me what he told you and we can go from there?'

'No, no.' He shook his head. 'I want to hear it from you.'

'Hear what exactly?' I knew what he meant. I felt the visceral panic of prey unwittingly lowered into the lion's den.

'Son, I'm here to help you.'

'I told my dad last week that I'm gay.'

'OK!' He seemed encouraged by the progress. 'Now, who told you that you are gay?'

Maureen came to mind. I feared that they would try to blame her, but she hadn't told me I was gay. I had told her.

'What do you mean? Nobody told me.'

'Then how do you know?'

'Sorry?'

'How can you be certain?'

I was pretty sure he didn't want the intimate details.

'I ... I ...' I had no answer. How did I know? It was just a part of me. How did straight people know?

'It's like, how do you know if you're left-handed? No one tells you, do they, Uncle? You just ... know.'

'I can help you.'

Five years ago I would have bitten his hand off. I would have been desperate enough to try anything. And he would have been able to feed off that desperation, abuse my vulnerability to bend me into willing submission. But it wasn't five years ago any more and it wasn't my desperation but my parents' that he now sought to exploit.

'I have helped others,' he added.

'Others?'

'Yes, I have helped many young Muslims who think they are like this,' he said. This was no real doctor but a man who peddled stories of black magic and jinn possession.

'You've helped people?' I was beyond the point of believing there was a cure. The lawyer in me was kicking in, ready to cross-examine him on the evidence in support of this preposterous claim. 'As in, you've had young men and women tell you they are gay?'

He flinched at the word. 'Yes. Mostly men.'

'And now, after your help, they tell you they are no longer gay?' Each time I said the word *gay*, I emphasised it, poking at his disgust.

'Yes, exactly. And I can help you too.'

Adrenaline surged through me. I had switched into fight or flight mode.

'They are lying to you,' I said, between gritted teeth.

'How do you know?' he said.

'I just do. They are lying to you and you are making them more miserable with your promises.' We stopped walking. The whispering trees seemed to close in around us.

'I speak the truth, son.' I wanted him to stop calling me *son*. 'I am helping them.' This man was going round the country telling young Muslims they could be cured of their Western 'disease'. He was causing unspeakable harm. 'This thing does not exist,' he told me. 'It is an invention of the West.'

'Is that what you've told my parents? If it doesn't exist, how are you able to cure it?'

'Good question. Well done, I'm glad you are asking. It is simply in your mind.'

'Whether or not it is in my mind doesn't make it any less real. How can you help me?'

'Excuse me?' He didn't appreciate my assertiveness.

'You've said that you cure these people and you can cure me so please just tell me how,' I asked impatiently.

'Not yet. Not when you are speaking to me in this tone.'

'What tone?! You've told me you can cure me so tell me how and then I can make a decision about whether to go along with it or not.'

'It is not your decision alone. You have to respect your father's wishes too.'

'Please leave him out of this. You have already given him enough false hope.'

'Why are you so convinced it is false?'

Nothing I said was landing, making any difference to his arguments. If I'd been in court, my client would have been appalled that I was unable to outmanoeuvre a witness who so clearly lacked any credibility.

'Are you gay?' I asked.

'What? Am I what?' He was incredulous.

'Are you gay?' I repeated.

'You have no manners whatsoever!'

'I apologise,' I said. 'Now answer the question. I've answered your questions. Are you gay?'

'Of course not! You stupid boy.' I had hit a nerve.

'OK. So then you don't know, do you?'

'Know what?' He was confused.

'You can't possibly know whether these people who claim to be cured are lying to you because you aren't gay yourself. I am gay and I can tell you that it can't be cured.' By now, I was feeling a mixture of anger and exasperation. 'What your "patients" tell you is almost certainly only what they want you to hear because it is what they want their families to hear.'

'You are the most stubborn young man I have ever met!'

As we marched home in silence, he walked slightly ahead of me, and I mentally high-fived myself for finding a corner to back him into. I thought about how sanctimonious I had been about English families not being close, without acknowledging the consequences of being too close. I had saved my family from years of lies. Years of awkward conversations and meetings with unsuitable matches. Years of embarrassment each time their overly fussy son said no to yet another young woman whose parents they would have to call and inform.

It felt like this was a pivotal moment in my relationship with my parents. I loved them so much, but right then I despised them. I loathed that, undoubtedly against their better judgement, they had put themselves through this charade of finding a cure, put Abbass through it, but most of all, that they did not have the parental instinct to protect me from it.

'Your son is a very difficult young man. He is refusing to listen to what I have to say,' Dr Saab reported back to my dad in the living room.

'I have listened and you are lying to everyone!'

'Mohsin!' My dad was affronted by my manners in front of this elder. 'Please leave us for a moment.'

He and Dr Saab spoke in low voices and then I was summoned back into the room.

'Mohsin, Dr Saab has drops for you.' He held up a small brown bottle. 'If you put some in your drink every day then eventually you will be cured.' He smiled at me lovingly, as if he had found the answer to all our problems and all I had to do was drink this magic potion. 'Of course you have to stay at home and er ... not go out, all right?'

He was asking for celibacy, at least until the cure had kicked in. Then I could go on a rampage, I assumed. The love in his eyes was disarming.

Perhaps all the ointment amounted to was an invisibility cloak that didn't actually work but allowed the family to deny the gayness and collectively pretend it wasn't there any more. Or maybe it contained some form of chemical castration. Fuck that, I thought.

'Dad, you are the very reason I cannot drink that,' I said, pointing to the bottle.

'What?' He frowned.

'The truth is that every day I take a sip is one more day that you live in hope that something will change, but it will not. I was born this way, I have always been this way and will always be this way.' My voice shook. It was as if I was having an out-of-body experience, as if from above I was looking down at this scene with despair for the young man in the room. I was unable to hold myself together much longer. I realised now why my mum had no part to play in this. She had resigned herself to the inevitable misfortune that I would always be this way, whereas my dad was still buoyed by the hope of a cure.

The revelation of my sexuality was like an earthquake that had ripped apart the ground we stood on, them on one side and me on the other. I considered leaving them there, to find my own way. A life without them that was free of judgement and free from guilt. But imagining them standing together on the other side of the crater, I knew I couldn't let them go, even if that's what they wanted.

30

I was twenty-four years old when I started working as a lawyer. At Linklaters, I became one of the scurrying suits in the City we drove past as children. The people my dad pointed out as bankers and lawyers with a hint of admiration in his voice. Soon after I started, I contacted my old comprehensive school and told them I wanted to help. It was 2009 and, in the eight years since leaving, education had transformed my life. I felt a sense of responsibility towards the school that was difficult to articulate. I wanted kids like me, living hand to mouth in one of the richest cities in the world, to look at those suits not only with admiration but with ambition.

Abbass was taking another big step in life. He was getting married the following year. Or at least I hoped he was. He hadn't yet disclosed my sexuality to his bride-to-be. She had to willingly join a family tarnished with the shame of a gay son because, once she was a part of it, it would become her shame too.

'And what if she says she can't accept it? Or her parents won't?' I asked Abbass. The conversation placed our relationship on a tightrope, from which it seemed to me it would undoubtedly fall.

'Well then, that's that, I guess. You're my brother. I can't be with someone who doesn't accept you,' he said with a shrug.

I was moved by his unwavering loyalty. Abbass had seen her at a family wedding, weddings I tended to avoid because I felt like an outsider even though no one treated me as such. Theirs wasn't quite a *love marriage* but close enough. They had seen each other, liked each other and he had asked her parents for her hand. After a few conversations, she agreed. The phrase *love marriage* was uniquely South Asian, and existed because the default was a union organised entirely by one's parents. The term used to suggest mischievous defiance although nowadays the practice was becoming more acceptable.

'When will you speak to her?' I asked.

'Tonight,' he said.

Abbass knew how much I liked his fiancée. She seemed kind and decent. If she couldn't live with the idea of a gay brother-in-law would there be other brides for Abbass? Might he spend his life coming out of my closet only to be rejected too? I didn't want him to be shunned, but the only way to hide who I was from the woman he married was to hide from him, and it was already too late for that.

'She said she already knew,' Abbass told me later that evening.

I was sure my heart had stopped beating. Gossip in our community spread like bushfire.

'Don't worry, it wasn't from the mosque. She said you don't look at her the way most men do.' He smiled. 'She said she can't wait to have a gay brother-in-law.'

Not marrying before my younger brother meant my family would have some explaining to do. I applied for a six-month transfer to Linklaters' Madrid office for summer 2010. As wedding fever began to build, I could feel a fever rising in me too. I'd be in London for the festivities but would fly away the minute they were over. It was in the aftermath that attention would turn back to me and my choices.

'Will it be a big wedding?' a colleague asked.

'No, not too big,' I said.

'I prefer it to be honest. I had a small wedding,' he said.

'I think having too many people could be overwhelming and very expensive,' I said.

'Yes, totally. Even eighty people felt like a lot.'

'Eighty?'

'Yes. How many is your brother having?'

'Around 300,' I said.

'*What?* I thought you said he was having a small wedding.'

'That is a small wedding. Eighty people would just about cover the cousins.'

As the elder brother, it was my responsibility to help plan the wedding and I did so willingly. I wanted Abbass to have the celebration I never would. I imagined having a partner, maybe even a life partner, but marriage to me meant family. It meant Islam and culture. I didn't want the bones and skin of what remained after the heart and soul were cut away.

'This one is beautiful!' my auntie said before switching to Urdu to ask the shopkeeper the price and recoiling instantly when he told her.

'Try it on,' she said.

'No ... I don't think ... I mean ...' I looked at my mum.

'Come on, Mohsin. We can take a picture and send it to Abbass. You think he'll like it, right?' my auntie said. It was a potential wedding outfit for my brother.

'I'm not sure he needs to ...' My mum tried to intervene. I wasn't sure if she was trying to protect me or herself.

'Just try it!' my auntie insisted.

It was a sherwani, a knee-length coat with buttons that ran from the neck to the waist. We were in an area of London heaving with Pakistani wedding shops. There were advantages to having a gay son, even if my mum couldn't acknowledge them.

The coat was dark cream with a Nehru collar embroidered with elaborate gold stitching. I pulled on the pencil-thin white trousers, and placed a deep purple turban on my head.

'Mashallah!' my auntie shouted. I secretly liked to watch videos of gay couples proposing or getting married. I imagined, just for a moment, wearing this outfit in one such video.

I smiled at my mum. She seemed transfixed by the sight of me in these clothes. She smiled back briefly but then turned towards the rail of clothes she had been rifling through. In the mirror I stared at the person I should have been and considered the life I had been forced to give up. My mum and I quietly mourned the same loss, but to her it was all my fault.

My parents had erected a marquee in their garden, and every night during the run-up to the wedding, we had friends and family over. Uncle Tier and his wife had promised to dance to Justin's Bieber's 'Baby' and we took a short break from Bollywood music to insist he show us his signature moves. Within minutes everyone was clapping and dancing. After the song was over, he whispered in my ear, 'I'll do the same at your wedding, Mohsin.'

'Ha! Then I'm not sure you'll get an invite,' I replied.

My dad, more introverted in a crowd, took a seat at the far end of the marquee, until someone handed him a microphone and he began to sing. I'd all but forgotten he had a great voice. He sang an old love song that he and my mum both remembered fondly.

Love was this intangible feeling the world wrote eulogies to, sang about, pined after. The obsession with love perplexed me. I had learned to control my emotions, and love was, allegedly, the opposite of self-control. My experiences had hardened me to its soft touch. Another type of touching, though, I was becoming more familiar with.

Madrid had a vibrant gay scene and threw me into the deep end of dating. Now back in London thinking of my new life in Spain, I understood that something had shifted within me. I was no longer disgusted with myself. I smiled at the memory of the dates I'd been on and the guys I'd been with. I thought fondly of my life in Madrid and couldn't wait to return after the wedding. I'd spent all this time worrying that I was in free fall, but now I realised I was flying.

The beat of the dhol, the Indian drum, commanded the attention of spectators on the north and south banks as it rang out over the Thames. A boat from Mississippi sailing down an English river to celebrate a Pakistani wedding. Abbass and his wife made their way to the top deck, towards the stage where their thrones awaited. As usual, the format of Pakistani weddings dictated that the couple, married in a much smaller ceremony earlier, be seated on a raised platform in front of the feasting tables. Although the couple could speak to each other occasionally, their role was to sit still as their three hundred, mostly unfamiliar, guests looked on. Abbass resembled a young Mughal prince in the sherwani we had chosen for him but, as with most cultures, his bride was the focus.

Her pink-and-gold lehnga, consisting of a floor-length skirt, matching top and long scarf affixed to the back of her head, framed the perfect Pakistani bride: fair skin, long black hair and a timid demeanour. The last was key. If she smiled too much, it was disrespectful to the family she was leaving. If she cried for too long, she was offending the one she was joining. Although it was OK for Abbass to dance, it would be immodest for her to do the same. I had been at a Pakistani wedding once where the bride joined the groom for one dance. Watching her assert her place made the crowd erupt with joy. Things were slowly changing, I hoped.

'God, you've got so big! Mashallah,' one auntie said, clasping my cheeks in her hands.

'I haven't seen them in years – your boys are so tall, so handsome.' My mum smiled proudly. 'Tell me, why aren't you married yet?' she asked.

It was a question we quietly anticipated and yet it still rendered us both mute. At least for a moment. And that moment was all it took for the unspoken thing to lodge itself between my mum and me. I wanted to reach for her hand, tell her it was OK, that we were in this together. But I worried she would pull away.

It was only a matter of time before my extended family and parents' friends discovered the truth, if they didn't know already. Fortunately, I'd invited twenty of my own friends to the occasion, to act as a buffer between me and the whispering crowd.

While it remained unspoken, my parents knew I would never marry, so this was my only opportunity to involve my friends in our traditions. It had been Mum and Dad who suggested I invite them; the gesture made me wonder whether they knew how hard the wedding might be for me, an insight that seemed to have been absent up until then.

I felt an immense sense of excitement for Abbass's future, his family, his children. Although I tried to set aside my own problems, I was consumed with emotion. Looking at my brother, I felt a yearning for a life I would never live. I saw the pride and simple happiness in my parents' eyes as they gazed at him and envied his ability to inspire such devotion. He was making their dreams come true.

My dad drove me to the airport so that I could catch my flight back to Madrid. The small henna tattoo from the mehndi celebration, of my name written on my wrist in Urdu script, had slowly begun to dim just like my memories of the wedding. I was feeling devastated at having had to watch the life I wanted play out before me. I was an extra in a story and now I had no story of my own. My dad took my hand and I hoped he might never take it away. He had tears in his eyes too. He knew why this was so hard, why I had to leave and why I didn't want to. Although he still maintained I should see a medical doctor about my sexuality, I had never loved him so much. My dad had once said that he was relieved when each of us was born. He did want a daughter but feared her wedding day. The day that he would have to say goodbye because, according to our culture, she was of another family now. He couldn't bear the thought of raising a child only to watch her leave. I wasn't joining another family but it felt like I was leaving mine. I might not be a girl, but he was losing me too.

31

After Madrid I returned to the Linklaters London office and moved back home. Abbass and his wife were living there too because that was tradition. While my sexuality was an unwelcome subject in the house so was any suggestion that I move out. Before, I was two people. Now I was one but living in two worlds. The first was the world of the dutiful son, who had recently returned to working long hours in his big law firm. The second was the world of the young gay man, whom the family often glimpsed returning from a night out, as they rose from their beds before sunrise to eat before a day of Ramadan fasting. It was like passing each other on adjacent escalators, moving in opposite directions.

I'd come out of the closet but they wanted to throw me back in. It was too late though. I was older now and more comfortable in my skin, more easily able to own my sexuality and integrate it into the whole, even into the Asian part. The problem was, no one else seemed to think the two belonged together. Unlike many other bars, gay venues were a melting pot of different classes, but my race still seemed to invite only a begrudging acceptance.

'Sorry, mate, it's members only,' the bouncer said to me.

'I've been here before,' I said.

'Like I said, *members* only.'

'Look, I've been here a few times. I'm meeting friends inside,' I said.

'You know it's a gay bar, right? I don't want any trouble.'

'Yes, I know. I'm gay.'

'OK, in you go.'

*

Inside, the jingle bells began to chime. '*All I want for Christmas is youuuuuuuuuuuuuu.*' The Mariah Carey song blasted over the club's sound system, and the partygoers let out a collective scream.

'OMG. He is so damned sexy,' my friend said. I looked over at a topless guy dancing nearby. 'He literally doesn't have a hair on him. If I was that sexy I'd just stay at home touching myself,' he added.

Talk of hairless bodies made me feel like each hair of mine was on display. These pale guys all looked like they had alopecia from the neck down. The ideal gay, it seemed. I'd grown up bombarded with images like this that inadvertently dictated what I once thought made a man beautiful. How could I blame anyone else for the prejudice we had all been fed?

'Oh, what about him?'

'Yeah, he's fit,' I said.

'Go say hi.'

'No! I'm too scared –'

'Gurl, you ain't scared of anything!' he said, shoving me in the direction of the young guy in the polo shirt. He might be right, I thought. My confidence had grown immensely after Madrid.

'Hi,' I said.

'Hi,' he replied, with barely a cursory glance in my direction.

'I'm Mohsin.'

'Sorry, you aren't my type.'

'Oh, OK … sure … no problem …'

'Nothing personal. I just prefer English guys.'

I returned to my friend.

'What'd he say?'

'Has a boyfriend,' I said, shrugging. 'Why the hell are they playing this song anyway?' I yelled over Mariah's voice, trying to change the subject.

'Why not?'

'Because it's June,' I said.

He looked at me, shrugged and shouted, 'I love being gay!'

I hoped I might fare better with Internet dating but the excitement of being able to meet someone with a few simple clicks soon wore off. 'No Asians' was common, sometimes, even, 'no Pakis'. Each time I read that, the words made me feel just a little less attractive and a little more isolated. All these messages made me sure that every gay man wanted a white knight in shining armour. I envied my mum for being able to pass for Caucasian. It seemed like the perfect disguise for the gay world.

'Well, yes, my family is Muslim,' I said to my date.

'Isn't it just awful about Isis throwing gays from the top of buildings?' he said, taking me somewhat by surprise.

'Yes it is,' I said. Should I be apologising? I wondered. 'You know that at no point in Islamic history has anyone been punished for homosexuality until Isis? And that there is a direct correlation between the rise in homophobia in Muslim countries and colonisation?'

'Do your parents know you're gay?' he asked.

I had come to loathe this question, especially because it always seemed to come up on a first date. It was personal and a simple yes was never enough.

'Yes, but let's save that story for date number two,' I said, knowing there wouldn't be one. He smiled. I smiled back.

'You know, I've figured out why you're so sexy. You have Western features and brown skin,' he announced. 'It's that combination of East and West.'

'You think that without my "Western features" I wouldn't be attractive?'

'That's not racist!'

'No?'

'Of course not. If I was racist I wouldn't be here, would I?' he said triumphantly.

For gays, I was too Muslim. For Muslims, I was too gay. For whites, I was too brown, and for my family, I was too white. It was time to create a space where I could just be myself. And to do that, I had to bite the bullet and move out of the house because it no longer felt like a home.

Just before the London 2012 Olympics, Abbass and his wife had a little girl. Looking at his tiny, precious daughter I remembered my conversations with Maureen and considered how I would treat a child of my own. I couldn't imagine feeling anything but love. I couldn't imagine placing any conditions upon that love. And I couldn't imagine shunning it in deference to the rules of culture and religion.

One of my mum's favourite films was called *Umrao Jaan*, a 1980s Bollywood classic that told the story of a young village girl who was kidnapped and sold into a life of prostitution. In the final scene the girl, now a young woman, unknowingly returns to her old village. During her dance for the pleasure of the village men she slowly begins to notice that her surroundings look familiar. She follows her memories back to her childhood home where her elderly mother still lives. Her mother, upon realising what her long-lost daughter has become, rejects her for bringing shame on the family. Every time my mum watched the scene she shed tears for this young woman forced out of her family through no fault of her own. Why could my mum show such deep empathy for this fictitious character but not for her own son?

My mum avoided making eye contact with me. In the solar system of my family, my mum was the sun yet I couldn't feel her warmth because her light did not reach me, could not reach me. My sexuality offended her deeply and so, by extension, did I. It was always in the room with us. It sat in the corner mocking my parents and poking fun at me. I began to feel the presence of the jinn again only because of the way my mum reacted to me: as if she could see it. She was meant to protect her son from the monsters but she had turned me into one instead.

I thought back to normal conversations between us, seemingly mundane stories she would recount after a day at school about how one of her young pupils had asked her what a nipple was or farted unbelievably loudly in the middle of reading time. I missed these easy, everyday exchanges.

If she was the sun, then I was the planet slowly drifting from its defined orbit towards a black hole. I had trained myself to feel very little about the way she reacted to me, there seemed no point in getting angry. I couldn't resolve her pain, so I looked away.

When I told her I was moving out she cried, but told me she understood all the same. Perversely, I was pleased to see her tears; they served as a reminder that, despite the turmoil between us, I was still her son. She still loved me. Even when I made it difficult for her to do so.

'Take care of Mum, OK?' I told Abbass.

'Oh, don't think you're getting out of it that easy. Just cos you're gay. Don't think you aren't pulling your weight,' he said.

'Well, it won't be long before we can put them in a home.'

'I heard that!' my mum said through the tissue that was held to her nose.

32

I was increasingly drawn towards the fight for social justice, as if it were an antidote to the injustice I felt with my family. The gap between the opportunities afforded to the people I'd gone to school with and the people I had been at university with seemed inconceivably wide. I set up an initiative at Linklaters to help young people from disadvantaged backgrounds become lawyers, but it didn't feel substantial enough. I wanted to use my legal training to address the important issues facing society, so I applied to the Supreme Court for a year-long placement to work with the most important judges in the country.

'Last question,' said one of the two judges on the other side of the desk.

I gulped. The last time I had applied I'd been rejected before the interview. It was surreal; usually such judges would be in grand chambers behind grand desks, beneath a royal coat of arms. Instead we were in a small room in the Supreme Court, overlooking Westminster Abbey, holding a conversation like ordinary people. And yet the stakes were high.

'Why didn't you get a first at university? I'm asking because your CV is strong but this is a competitive process and I want to give you the chance to elaborate.'

The question caught me completely off guard, although I should have expected it – after all, I was applying for one of seven places to be a judicial assistant to the justices of the Supreme Court, sitting at the apex of the British legal hierarchy. It wasn't unreasonable for them to probe any area that shed light on my intellect.

'Well ... honestly, I think it was a question of attitude rather than ability,' I said. I hoped they might understand that sometimes life is tough, that my experience was vastly different from the majority of those others they were interviewing. The road had been bumpy, but I didn't say any of that.

I was sure the interview had gone badly, so used my KFC Locator app to find the nearest KFC, and ate a whole family bucket meal. Later, when I received an email from the court offering me a place, my first reaction was utter elation followed hot on the heels by a pang of regret at the amount of fried chicken I'd eaten.

Although my family was pleased, I wasn't sure they completely understood just how special this opportunity was.

'How can you take a year out? Your firm will just let you go and then come back?' my mum asked.

'It's because of the prestige of working with the judges. It's like I'm a singer and I'm being offered the chance to sing with Beyoncé for a year,' I said.

'Beyoncé needs to pay you more!'

I worked closely with Judge Lord Wilson from the start, who expected me to meet him in his office at 9 a.m. each morning to discuss the day's upcoming case.

'Good morning, Mohsin,' he said in his cut-glass accent. He had thick, white, slicked-back hair and a wide smile.

'Good morning, Lord Wilson.' The court decreed that judicial assistants had to address the justices by their title, rather than their first name. It demonstrated respect for the institution.

'I've been invited to give a speech to the Medico-Legal Society at Queen's University in Belfast,' he said. I stared at him blankly. 'A group of Northern Irish lawyers,' he explained. 'Given my background in family law, I'd like to make a speech on gay marriage and I'd like your help.'

I froze, wanting the floor to open up and suck me in.

'Yes, of course. What can I do?'

'Well, as you know, gay marriage is not yet legal in Northern Ireland.'

'Yes.'

'Well, I'd like to illustrate how ridiculous this is through historical and current examples of marriage. I want to show that the concept was man-made and can therefore be adjusted by man.'

I wanted to come out to him right there and then but it was irrelevant and, more to the point, unprofessional.

'Of course, Lord Wilson. I'll get to work straight away.'

The speech went through at least twenty-four drafts and each draft brought with it more queries to resolve and quirky examples to find. During the course of working on the speech, I noticed Lord Wilson's formidable literacy didn't extend to computers so I lent him my new iPad in an effort to demonstrate how easy they were to use. Two days later he had acquired his own. It was the first time he would have an email address.

Every minute of working on the speech taught me something new; I was doing something that mattered. Lord Wilson effortlessly, politely and humorously dismantled the arguments levelled against gay marriage by using examples throughout history of how human beings had changed the concept of marriage to suit themselves. His ability to sculpt words into an attractive argument was akin to watching Michelangelo work with marble I imagined. The first time I read his concluding statement, I welled up.

> The most important benefit of same-sex marriage is the symbol that it holds up to the heterosexual community, not forgetting teenagers apprehensively trying to make sense of their own emerging sexuality, that each of the two types of intimate adult love is as valid as the other. The availability of marriage properly dignifies same-sex love. To the question 'why should same-sex couples, who can as civil partners already enjoy all relevant rights, be allowed to get married?', the proper response in my view is 'why shouldn't they?'

I had to pinch myself to make sure I wasn't dreaming. Not only did I have the most interesting job a young lawyer could do, but by extraordinary luck, I was also working on a project that held a deeply personal significance.

When he returned from his trip to Ireland, we celebrated in his office. 'Lord Wilson, aside from learning so much, there is another reason why I enjoyed working on the speech.'

'Oh?' he said.

'Well ... um ... actually ... I'm gay. I didn't tell you before because I thought it unprofessional, but now that the speech is over and we've been working together for a while I wanted to say how honoured I feel to have had the chance to work on it with you.'

He smiled with his characteristic warmth. 'Mohsin, I hope you won't mind my saying, but I already knew.'

'Oh?' I sat up straighter, uncrossing my legs.

'Yes – not because I could tell or anything,' he said hurriedly.

'Oh?' I seemed to have no other words in my vocabulary.

'Well ...' He paused long enough to make us both uncomfortable. 'You know when you lent me your iPad?'

'Yes ...'

'Well, you might recall that I returned it to you rather hastily?' I nodded. 'You see, these rather colourful messages kept popping up from a young man called *Alejandro* ...' It suddenly occurred to me that my iPad was synced with my phone. 'Of course I tried not to read them but they were rather insistent ...'

OH. MY. DEAR. GOD. I opened my mouth to speak, but all that came out were the stuttering noises of shame. He had read naughty messages between me and a fiery Spanish guy I'd met on a night out.

'Now, Mohsin, there is absolutely nothing to be embarrassed about and I do hope you don't mind me having said something but I thought it better to be truthful.'

'Yes ... of course. Um ... if you'll excuse me ... I have to ... go,' I said before darting out of the room.

A little later, I returned to his office and we laughed about it. That laughter pierced the thick layer of formality between us. Once upon a time, an incident like this would have left me desperate and ashamed but not any more. Living a truthful life meant I could be less careful with my secrets. It meant I could just laugh. And Lord Wilson wasn't the only judge to embrace the whole of me. I had expected to suppress parts of myself to fit in, but the entire Supreme Court welcomed me for who I was.

Earlier that same year, the Marriage (Same-Sex Couples) Act 2013 had passed. When I celebrated that important victory in the battle for equality, I still couldn't picture same-sex marriage for myself, although working on the speech with Lord Wilson had stirred my imagination.

I told my parents about the speech and used it as an opportunity to mention that I might get married one day and might even have children. My mum looked winded by the suggestion, as if I'd punched her in the stomach. Her expression left me feeling as though things between us hadn't changed very much at all in the seven years since I had come out to her. But then one of the court's cases made headlines.

The TV anchor reported that a Christian couple were taking their fight all the way to the Supreme Court, which would decide whether they were justified in turning a gay couple away from the bed and breakfast they ran.

'Are you involved in this case?' my mum asked.

'Yes – the hearing's just started.'

'These people refused to let the ... couple stay?' she asked.

'It's a little more complicated than that, but essentially: yes. They were refused a double room.'

She paused, thinking. 'Well, that's not right,' she said eventually. 'It's none of their bloody business!' It was as if she was picturing me being chased from the B&B; she was outraged. And just like that, a small stream of sunlight had burst through the tiniest of cracks.

Lord Wilson and I became ever closer over time. He surprised me, my family, but most of all my lawyer friends by turning up to my birthday dinner in a BYOB east London curry house, where the food was delicious and the decor simple. We came from completely different backgrounds. He was one of the most senior judges in the country, double my age – and my boss. It was the most unlikely of places to find friendship and yet there it was.

A few months later, Lord Wilson and his wife were coming to my parents' house for tea.

'Mum went to WHITErose for tea and cakes,' Abbass added.

'Of course I did! It's not every day you have a Lord and Lady come to your house,' she said.

'How would you like your tea?' Mum asked our guests.

'Just a splash of milk, thanks,' said Lord Wilson.

'I'll make it easier,' she said. Don't do it, I thought. 'Which of our skin colours would you like your tea to be? I prefer mine the colour of Raza but for some people that's too much milk.' Mum laughed, but she was right. The five members of my family were all different skin tones; she was the fairest, my dad the darkest and the rest of us in between. It was actually a really helpful way of gauging how much milk a guest would take in their tea. Without a moment's pause, Lord Wilson replied, 'Well, OK. I think I'd quite like it that colour,' he said, pointing at me, grinning.

I was approaching the end of my year at the Supreme Court and getting ready to return to my desk at Linklaters. The court's Pakistani guards loved the idea of one of their own working upstairs rather than down, they said.

I had been asking them all year and, as a farewell gift in our last week, one guard agreed to take me and the other assistants to the top of the court's stone tower that dominated the west side of Parliament Square. From the stone parapets it felt like the whole of London was laid out before me. I stood at the pinnacle of the British establishment facing Parliament, Westminster Abbey, the London Eye and, beyond that, the Shard. From where I was standing, however, I could no longer see the London I had grown up in.

33

Now that I didn't live with my family, my mum and I became good at pretending our relationship wasn't fractured beyond repair. The distance helped. Raza, now seventeen, knew nothing about me and we kept it that way. The new normal was for us to talk as strangers. It became normal for me to say I was going out for a meal or going on holiday and for them not to ask where or with whom. Subjects such as marriage, children, and the future were icebergs we had to steer clear of. Icebergs that only began to melt after the news of a Pakistani family, just like ours, who had crashed straight into one with *Titanic* consequences.

'HARLEY STREET DOCTOR DIES AFTER FALLING NAKED FROM FLAT' read the headline on 1 August 2014. His body had apparently been on the street in plain sight for hours after he fell four storeys from his balcony. The paper identified him as Nazim Mahmood. This Pakistani doctor was about my age, and gay. A knot formed in my stomach. He was pronounced dead at the scene and, according to the newspaper report, his death was not being treated as suspicious. The knot tightened. Not suspicious? This had to be about his sexuality, I thought.

Googling him revealed nothing about the man and his life. Months later another headline appeared, following the inquest into his death: 'DOCTOR KILLED HIMSELF AFTER MOTHER ASKED HIM TO SEEK "GAY CURE".' My curiosity was reignited.

Reading more about Nazim's life and his death, I wondered how it was possible to feel such affinity with someone I had never met, would never know. According to the reports, Nazim had hidden his sexuality from his family for many years and escaped to London to live more freely. He took his own life shortly after coming out to his mum. Each detail plunged me further into a state of despair. Despair for a community that refused to accept the reality of homosexuality. Despair for its young people, who would go through life hating themselves for the way they were born. And despair for Nazim and his family, his life having been needlessly cut short.

That night I went to my parents' house, walking in to find Mum performing the cleaning ritual before prayer. As I watched her cup her hands up to God and whisper her wishes to him, I was surprised by the pang of jealousy that rushed over me. I no longer resented Islam because I could see now that it was not to blame. Looking at my mum, I felt guilty for all I had put her through, and all that was still to come.

'Mochie, I need to talk to you.'

'OK.'

'Did you see the story about that doctor?'

'His name was Nazim, Mum.'

'I kept the article. I tried to throw it away, but I couldn't.' She looked down at her hands in her lap. 'You know that I love you very much, don't you?'

'I do.'

'And you know that I would never want anyone to hurt you or ...' she looked at me now, '... you to hurt yourself?'

'I know, Mum. You don't have to worry about that. Maybe once but not any more.'

She looked away again. I'd heard about a meeting for South Asian parents with LGBT children and I decided now was the time.

'Mum ... there's this meeting for Asian parents. Parents with children like me.' I saw a small window of opportunity and threw myself through it. It felt unfair of me to use her reaction to Nazim's death in this way, but I had to try.

'OK, let's go!' she said. Her appearance had the sheen of a calm river. The water was still, and the trees along the riverbank perfectly reflected on the surface. But looking more closely, I could see small currents passing through the water.

'My daughter is now doing her second master's,' the woman said, holding a half-eaten homemade samosa in one hand.

'My son just finished his PhD so now he is a doctor. He also cooks very well. He made these samosas himself. Delicious no?' said another in a thick Indian accent.

We were in the kitchen of the offices of a charity hosting the event for parents of LGBT South Asians. It was a potluck event, so each attendee brought some food along. Ours was the only contribution that wasn't home-made because, until the last moment, my mum wasn't sure she could go through with it.

'Shall I drop the Oxford bomb?' my mum whispered to me.

'You know, I was so upset when she told me,' said the woman with the samosa.

'Yes, I was also very, very upset,' replied the other.

'But now I see that this is normal. I love her completely!'

'Yes, yes, me too, completely normal.'

Asian mothers could compete over absolutely anything.

As parents and their offspring took their seats in the circle of chairs, I scanned the room for any sign of a Muslim family. I recognised the

Hindus from the red bindi painted in the middle of their foreheads and there was a Sikh father with a turban.

But by the end of the introductions it was clear that we were the only Muslims. My heart sank. I could feel my mum seizing up at the thought that there were almost two billion Muslims on the planet, more than a million in London, and she had to be the one to end up with a gay son. I feared the fallout, but hoped the discussion would salvage some of this potential wreckage.

'OK, first question!' The host held a small box with pre-submitted questions. 'What is the best thing about having a gay child?' he said, before answering: 'Well, we are FABULOUS, of course!' I took a deep breath. The ensuing discussion was entirely positive and entirely unhelpful. People talked about how wonderful their children were and how sad it was that bigoted members of the South Asian community couldn't see that.

'I'm sorry, but I have a problem with it. And I don't think that makes me bigoted,' my mum said.

The group fell silent.

'I love my son but I was raised to believe this is wrong. I know none of you are Muslim but I think your religions might say similar things, and if they don't, then our culture does, doesn't it? I think it's fantastic that you can embrace your children the way that you have, but how did you get to that point? I'm here because I want to talk about how hard it is.'

Four sentences. Four whole sentences from my mum on my sexuality. When I was younger these words might have upset me. But with the passage of time, I came to understand that it almost didn't matter what she said. It mattered that she had said something. This was an indication that she was willing to face her demon, to face me, and once she could look it in the eye, maybe, just maybe, she could defeat it.

Sitting opposite me in the dentist's waiting room in east London were three British Bengalis: a boy and two girls in their late teens. One of the girls wore a hijab. The boy's Arsenal football shirt made me think of Raza. I imagined him sitting around with his friends, gossiping the way these three were. It was a side of him that, as his grown-up big brother, I rarely saw.

'You know that group, "England4English" came down here for some march. Fuckin' dickheads calling us Pakis ... I was like, *bruv, you in the wrong part of town, we from Bangladesh here, you chump,*' the boy said.

'Dey so dumb ... Stupid racist chavs,' said one of the girls.

I zoned out of their conversation, thinking of Raza again. Hoping that he was as indifferent to the threat from racist thugs as these three appeared to be. When I zoned back in, they were huddled around the boy's phone looking at a message.

'Black sheep of the family? He's lucky even to be a sheep!' the boy said, flanked on either side by his friends. From what I could piece together, the message was about a Bengali boy who had come out to his family after his mosque had found out.

'Why was he even going to the mosque?' said the girl in the hijab.

'It's what they learn in school, innit? They teach them gay rights. They're tryna make it normal, but it ain't,' said the other girl.

'It's disgusting. In my school there was a lesbian. Urgh.'

My hands shook with rage. The hypocrisy of it floored me. I wanted to shout at them, but what would that achieve? So much of the world was shouting and nobody seemed to hear anything any more. It wasn't comfortable to acknowledge but I'd once held similar prejudice.

Inside, the dentist confirmed that the pain in my jaw was the result of clenching my teeth at night. She asked if there was anything causing me to be anxious or feel stressed and, although I didn't tell her, I realised that my efforts with my family were taking their toll. I passed the three young people as I left. Then paused outside the surgery. I had to say something. I went back inside, but they were no longer in the waiting room. I grabbed a piece of paper and a pen and scribbled down a message.

Salaam, my younger sisters and brother,

I heard your conversation about 'England4English' (I'm sorry for listening in). I agree their racism is stupid. I loved what you said about it being dumb.

They hate us because we aren't white and they hate us because we pray differently from them. Do you know who else they hate? Gays. You described gays as disgusting. Just like race, it is dumb to judge someone based on their sexual orientation.

Islam teaches peace and tolerance. I know that there is much goodness in each of you. I'm not asking for acceptance but, please, don't be disgusted by something that I cannot choose. You are better than them and their hatred.

With much respect,

Mohsin

I left the note at reception and hurried off. I needed movement. I needed to feel things were happening in the world. I heard that London Pride was advertising for a volunteer legal director to join its board. I applied and was appointed. I'd become the boy in the blue T-shirt my mum thought she saw online years ago. But that wasn't enough. I needed movement in my family too. I couldn't let Raza become one of those young people. I had to get to him before prejudice set in.

'You can't tell him,' my dad said. He and my mum sat at the kitchen table while I stood. 'Not yet,' he added. My mum said nothing.

'He's seventeen years old. He's old enough and I don't want to lie to him any more. Besides, he probably already knows. He's not stupid,' I said.

'He won't be able to take it. He has exams coming up. What if he fails them?'

'Dad, Raza is not going to fail his A levels because I've told him about me.' Even now, in this moment of extreme frustration, I avoided the *gay* word. I was still trying to make myself and my language less abrasive to them. But I had to tell Raza.

Although I had never yelled at my parents at that moment I wanted to. I held back, reminding myself how isolated they must feel. I'd left my community, but I had found another. They did not have this option. They couldn't tell some of their siblings, their living parents, nor their network of friends. I had an instinctive need to protect them, which made it difficult to get angry.

I'd spoken to Maureen a few times about telling Raza and she agreed that it was my decision. She also thought it was positive that Abbass was on board. It was, although it hadn't been easy to get him there.

'You drop bombs and then you leave, Mohsin. I get it. You have to leave, but you don't have to stick around to pick up the pieces. I do. And I have my own family now.' He was right. Since coming out, Abbass was now the de facto eldest son. They relied on him more than they did me, called upon him more than they did me and found it easier to love him. I saw his point but I hoped that telling Raza would lighten his burden too.

Abbass had recently moved out of my parents' home to a place about five minutes away. He brought Raza over to his house where I was waiting with my sister-in-law in their living room.

'Why are you all acting so weird?' Raza asked.

Looking at this tall young man in his Arsenal hoodie, it was difficult to reconcile this image with the baby whose nappies I'd once changed. I'd not been nervous of his reactions before that moment. Raza was a good boy though. The kind who willingly offered his seat to strangers on the Tube. The first time I saw him do this, I was proud of the way my parents had raised us.

'Raza, there's something I have to tell you ...' My voice wavered. Abbass sat across from us, fiddling with his hands.

'OK ...'

'It doesn't change anything and we are still the same family we have always been,' I said hurriedly, but really, I was stalling. Why hadn't I thought about how to say these words to him before?

I took a deep breath and looked at him.

'I'm gay.'

'I know.'

'What? Why didn't you say?'

'I just ... I just didn't really know what to say. Like, I had a feeling and then I figured Mum and Dad must be stressing at you. I guess I thought I'd just wait until you or Abbass told me.' He smiled, his eyes lighting up. 'I wear rainbow laces because of you.' The multicoloured laces were the symbol of a national campaign to make football more LGBT-inclusive.

His reaction took me and my parents by surprise. Raza's attitude seemed, in an instant, to demonstrate to them that the world might not collapse at the news. In my eagerness to circumvent Raza's prejudice, I had not considered that he had none. The young people in the dentist's waiting room had scared me. But they weren't the future. Raza was.

34

Now that I was living honestly with every member of my immediate family it was easier to live honestly with myself too. I had entered the world of corporate law because that was what was expected of me. With my thirtieth birthday fast approaching, I had to make decisions about where *I* wanted to go. I had always longed to be a barrister but never before had the resources or the confidence. Now I gathered my courage and resigned from my highly paid job at Linklaters to start training as a criminal barrister at 6KBW, the country's foremost criminal chambers. It seemed madness to leave the gilded corporate law lifestyle for the crumbling criminal courts, but it was also the most excited I had felt in a long time.

Becoming a barrister was the hardest thing I'd ever done professionally. Getting a place to train was highly competitive, with only a couple of hundred annual places available nationally and even fewer at the prestigious chambers in London. But that was just the beginning. The training process was like being rigorously interviewed for a whole year: I would be tested on how I wrote, how I spoke, how I dressed and how I thought.

Advocates are a lot like singers. Both professions require powerful voices. Both feature individuals who work very hard to become technically brilliant at their craft and both require auditions. Pupillage felt like an *X Factor* audition that lasted a year, but instead of one Simon Cowell there were fifty, and instead of singing one song, I sang hundreds.

The excitement of my new job quickly morphed into astonishment. As a trainee, I started in the lower courts dealing with less serious crimes, where the barristers didn't wear wigs and gowns. In my suit I was regularly mistaken by the court staff for the defendant. That might have upset me, if I hadn't seen the actual black and brown defendants routinely sentenced more harshly than the white. 'This is more like the Wild West,' one colleague explained. 'A jury trial in the Crown court – now that's where the proper court work happens.'

After a few months of experience in the lower courts, I was defending my first jury trial. Rising to give my closing speech, I realised I'd shrunk considerably. I had to jump above the desk just to make eye contact with the jury. They began giggling. I shouted at them to stop but my squeaky voice only made matters worse. I turned round to apologise to my client but he was pointing and laughing too. The judge was laughing so hard his wig fell off. I woke up in the middle of the night in a panic. My first jury trial was in a week's time. Whereas almost all other pupils had spent a year on a special course learning to be criminal barristers, I was going in blind because my qualification as a solicitor meant I was exempt from the course. The day arrived in what felt simultaneously like the blink of an eye and a thousand sleepless nights.

If doctors traded in human health, criminal barristers traded in human liberty. And someone else's liberty was in my hands.

As I crossed Tower Bridge, I could see the pyramid that sat at the top of the Canary Wharf skyscraper to the east, the same pyramid visible from my street as a child. A reminder of the life I had left behind. I feared I had taken a wrong turn. That my decision to forsake the big monthly salary in favour of what I called *meaning* had been too idealistic. But it was too late, at least for now.

Outside the eighties court building photographers with lenses as long as their arms snapped randomly at passers-by, testing their focus and angle, probably in anticipation of the arrival of a defendant or a witness in some high-profile case. Maybe an MP or an alleged murderer. Cases that would make the evening news. Cases unlike mine, in which my client was accused of assault. A fight that got out of hand.

'Excuse me, where's the barristers' robing room?' I asked the security guard.

'It's on the second floor but it's only for counsel,' he said.

'I am counsel. What's the code?'

'You're counsel?'

'Yes,' I said, questioning myself slightly, the way he was.

The robing room overlooked the Thames. It was littered with folders containing papers incomprehensible to the people they concerned. The room buzzed with morning chat about trials as barristers got dressed for court.

'So I stabbed him twice and you kicked him in the head while he was on the floor,' said a short woman to the man next to her, both in wig and gown.

'No, no, you stabbed him once, then I kicked him, but only in the stomach, then you stabbed him again,' the man replied.

'Are you certain of that?'

'Absolutely positive.' If not their attire, their plummy accents made it clear they were talking not about themselves but about their clients.

I inserted two brass studs into the collar of my specially designed white tunic shirt, one at the front and one at the back. I then attached them and the shirt to a thick-rimmed winged collar, its grip tight around my throat. I felt silly, not important, not debonair, not grand, just silly.

This tradition dated back to the 1600s and there were good reasons for keeping it, but it made me feel like I was playing dress-up in a game, rather than embarking on a fight to keep a man out of prison. For some people, it did the opposite. The game of life paused and the gravity of the criminal court process took them by the throat, literally. For me, the best argument for keeping the wig and gown was so that I wasn't constantly mistaken for the defendant, but I don't think that was the point.

I placed the black princetta gown over my shoulders, where it sat lightly, but the responsibility it represented did not. The green label inside read 'University Tailors, Anarkali, Lahore' in white writing. It was my grandfather's.

I removed the wig from the customary oval black tin box, my name in matt gold on the lid making it look more like a place for my ashes than for professional attire. I placed the wig on my head. Maureen had bought it for me as a gift to mark my becoming a barrister. It was the same ivory colour as the tower I was stepping into.

I glanced at myself in the mirror and was suddenly back at university, standing in my room in black tie. At that moment, I felt the same sticky unease, as if the clothes were too big for me or, in reality, I too small for them.

Now I was about to go down to the cells to meet someone who was locked up. My sense of discomfort heightened. If these clothes were so isolating to me, and I was wearing them, what must they be like for him? I'd made this point before and was asked whether hoodies and jogging bottoms might be preferable. Perhaps they would.

'Young man.' A voice at my back. 'Excuse me, young man,' he said again. I turned to face a barrister, in his sixties, only half dressed for court. 'I say, you don't happen to play cricket, do you? I'm looking for new players.' The other barristers in the room seemed to take a deep breath and hold it in.

'No, I'm sorry, I don't,' I said and left the room.

'Members of the jury,' I began my closing speech. I wanted to hit pause and enjoy the fact that I was saying these famous words to a jury, a real jury. I cleared my throat. It was silent for what felt like an uncomfortable length of time. The consequences of my speech would be serious, their impact making it difficult to speak the words. I took a sip of water and felt the eyes of the jury on me. As I did, the tail of my wig became stuck in the stud at the back of my shirt. It made me look like I had a stiff neck. After several attempts at subtly and gently untangling it, I tugged hard, ripping strands of the £500 horsehair wig from their delicate fastening. Barristers wore the wig and gown because it separated the individual from the role they were about to perform in the courtroom. For me, however, delivering the speech gave me a rush of adrenaline which seemed to take me closer to who I was rather than further away.

After I finished speaking I sat down and the jury retired. There was nothing to do then but wait for the outcome. I thought about my client, yet another poor young man caught up in the criminal justice system. He and I were from the same background and yet I was the lucky one, addressing the court rather than at its mercy. I reflected on the younger me fresh out of university. I wouldn't have lasted in this environment. Even if I'd had the money to go straight to the Bar, I would have lacked the confidence. The standards were created by and for an elite. I wasn't cut from the same cloth and had a choice: to pretend that I was of that ilk, or embrace the fact that I wasn't and personify the argument that there was room for difference.

'I wonder what they're doing in there. I'd really like to know,' I whispered to my opponent. She was a senior barrister who, knowing it was my first jury trial, guided me through the process. Her exceptional goodwill was actually not that exceptional. Although I'd been somewhat fixated by the pomp of the Bar, its personalities, regardless of background, proved that kindness had no class. There was a camaraderie among barristers, an invisible pillar, without which the justice system would wobble.

'Jury decisions are a bit like sausages. Probably best you don't know how they're made,' she said, smiling.

'Foreman of the jury, have you reached a verdict upon which you are all agreed?' the court clerk asked. I wasn't the defendant but I felt like I was in this with him. I knew what the outcome would be but maybe, just maybe …

'Yes. We find the defendant guilty.'

I was gutted. My client had received a fair trial and the evidence was against him. But I was still gutted. If this was how I felt when I thought it a just outcome, I couldn't imagine how I would feel if it were unjust. Perhaps I wouldn't have to; I was yet to learn if I had failed or passed the pupillage, and at that moment my confidence was wavering.

I had somehow made it to the end of the year-long, gruelling audition. It was an autumnal Saturday and barristers from my chambers had gathered for the meeting at which my application to become a proper barrister, a 'tenant', would be discussed. I was not invited to the meeting, which was a relief. I would rather eat my new horsehair wig than watch nearly fifty of London's top criminal barristers taking it in turns to tell the others what they thought of me.

'Hello,' I said.

'Mohsin, hi.' It was the voice of my pupil supervisor, a prominent QC, on the phone, a voice which always sent me into a state of minor panic. His brilliance, like that of so many barristers, was intimidating. Being taught by him felt like I was the blunt pencil and he the sharpener. 'I'll get straight to the point – you've made it. Well done. I'm pleased to tell you that the 2016 Annual General Meeting voted overwhelmingly in your favour and you are now a member of chambers.'

I'd made it, but the feeling wasn't like that of a champion racer taking the top stand. It was more of a struggling swimmer, who managed to reach land just before his arms gave up. But whatever it was, I'd made it.

35

Happy Valentine's Day! the preview to the message on my phone read. It was from a number I did not recognise. The prospect of it being from someone other than my mum sent a pinch of excitement through me. *GQ* magazine had voted 'criminal barrister' one of the top ten sexiest professions in the world but it didn't seem to be doing much for my love life. When I boastfully told people I was a barrister they assumed I was working in a coffee shop.

I opened the message and realised it was Pizza Hut Hackney, offering me a meal deal for two. I called the only valentine in my life, my nan, to say hello.

'So who is she then? Your real valentine?' she asked.

'You are,' I replied.

'No, no, no. When are you going to get married? I want to attend your wedding before I die,' she said. I wish I knew the answer. We spoke in Urdu, which had a funny way of making everything seem more dramatic than it needed to be.

'I want to attend my wedding before I die too,' I said.

A few weeks later, my phone pinged. *Hi, was really nice to meet you. Good luck in court today. Fancy going for a coffee sometime? Matthew PS Your client sounds guilty as hell. x*, the text message read. I'd met him at the weekend. He was Irish, six foot three, with ice blue eyes. Once upon a time I would have been too intimidated by his good looks to risk a 'hello', but by now I was so comfortable with the man I had become that it was enjoyable.

'So how can you defend someone if you know they're guilty?' Matthew asked. We sat next to each other on an old sofa, in an east London bar.

'Everyone asks that,' I said.

'Come on. If they're guilty, don't you feel bad for helping get them off?'

'You know the problem with that question? The people asking it never assume they'll be the ones in trouble,' I said. He seemed puzzled. 'Let's say I had to defend you.' I had the sudden urge to tell him that he'd have no problem in court, because the jury would take one look at his eyes and become as captivated by him as I was.

'Go on,' he said. I'd paused too long.

'Sorry. If you were in trouble and let's say you were innocent but all the evidence pointed to your guilt, would you want me to be your judge and jury?'

'I'd trust you,' he said, smiling.

'As long as you don't actually tell me you're guilty, my job in court is to be your advocate, your mouthpiece. It's not for me to judge.'

Matthew told me about growing up on the Irish border during the Troubles and I was embarrassed that, despite growing up nearby, I knew so little about it.

'Wait, seriously?'

'Yes,' he said.

'You actually played tennis over military roadblocks?'

He nodded. 'There were soldiers everywhere. Bomb scares in the cinema became so normal that we groaned about having to leave midway through the film. But, to be honest, that was the tail end of the troubles. My parents studied in England in the 70s. They got kicked off a bus once, just for being Irish.'

'Somebody shouted "Taliban" at my sister-in-law when she was walking down the street with my niece.' I said.

'We were yesterday's terrorists. You are today's. Anyway, the fighting has stopped but politics at home are still so messed up. Never mind gay marriage, you know women can't have abortions?'

'I know. I worked for this judge for a year and he gave a speech in Belfast about gay marriage. I'll send it to you if you like.'

'That would be great,' he said. 'You're on the board of London Pride too, right?'

'Oh, someone's been doing their research,' I said, intending to sound more playful than arrogant. Idiot, I thought to myself.

'Someone doesn't remember much from the night we met ... you told me,' he said. Massive idiot.

'Oh yes. It's like a volunteer job although it feels full-time. We get to walk at the front of the march though. You should join us,' I said. It was months away but I wanted to give him a reason to keep seeing me.

'When is it again?'

'July.'

'Oh, so you're pretty confident about this then?' he said, pointing at us both.

'Yeah, I guess I am.'

I volunteered with the board of London Pride because I realised that being gay meant being part of a community. Much like the one in which I had been raised, it had a history, customs and collective struggles against persecution. I had assumed that experience as one minority would make a person sympathetic to another. I knew this assumption was naive after having to explain more than once why 'Black Lives Matter' was not a racist movement and that pride essentially said the same thing but with queer lives. At times I felt like there was no room at the rainbow-coloured table for my shade of brown. Pockets of the community were wary of Muslims in particular. A wariness compounded by a murderous attack in Florida.

In June 2016, just before the London Pride march, there was a shooting in an Orlando gay bar and forty-nine, predominantly non-white, LGBT people were killed. The shooter pledged allegiance to Isis shortly before carrying out the attack. Reports indicated that he was motivated by a hatred of his own sinful sexual urges. I had felt this hatred once. Maybe if we weren't raised to hate ourselves it would be easier not to hate the world.

In July, Matthew joined me on the march. The moments spent with him felt like they might be building towards something bigger. His presence brought with it a stillness that, up until then, I had been unable to find in myself. A stillness that steadied even the pandemonium of a Pride march. We were also joined at the front by London's new mayor, Sadiq Khan.

Watching him, a straight Muslim man, stride among us, forty thousand people, in the aftermath of Orlando was as inspiring as the attack had been devastating. Sadiq was a hero to Muslims around the world. Pictures of him surrounded by drag queens and running up and down a huge rainbow flag flooded the Internet. I imagined a little Muslim boy, somewhere far away, seeing pictures of the London mayor and feeling a little less frightened of the future. I also made a point of sending the pictures to my family to show them that they were not alone.

The work I did for Pride was attracting attention and I wasn't sure what to do about it.

'What list?' Uncle Tier asked.

'It's a list of LGBT future leaders and I'm in the top twenty ... and it's going to be published in the *Financial Times*,' I said. 'They sent me an email letting me know in advance.'

'I see.'

'Yeah ... I mean, I'm clearly not one of the top twenty future leaders. It can't do any harm to my career, I guess. I told Mum and Dad but it didn't go too well.'

'You don't say!'

'They told me to use a pseudonym, which obviously doesn't make any sense. I told Dad I couldn't do that and he asked me if I'd get my name withdrawn from it.'

'It's difficult.' Uncle Tier sighed.

'It's been 10 years since I told mum. Most parents would be so happy for their son. You know I can't even enjoy it because I'm too worried about them.'

'I've already told your mum she has to accept you. Otherwise they will just be getting in your way and that won't work out well for them or for you.'

'So you don't think I should withdraw my name?'

'I think it's your decision, son. But you should consider how you are going to feel towards them if you did withdraw.'

In the end, I didn't withdraw my name but the achievement was bittersweet. Not being able to share my success with my family made me feel like it wasn't success at all. As though I'd been handed the keys to a stately home, walked inside and realised that, however grand it was, I needed someone to share it with. But the house wasn't really empty because, increasingly, Matthew was becoming the family I celebrated with.

*

'Mohsin.' My mum's voice was tearful. I could hear my dad, audibly upset in the background. I raced home to find my dad was huddled into a corner of the living-room sofa.

'Dad ... ?'

He wept as if his own child had passed away. She was like his own child. They had received word that morning that Mariam, the girl who my parents had once wanted me to marry, had been killed in a car crash. Dad flew to Pakistan the next day, underlining the lessons he taught me about friendship.

I mourned Mariam's passing, although I could not immediately appreciate her absence because we did not live in the same place or speak very much. It was an abstract mourning for something very real. A finality. The end of possibilities.

Closing my eyes, I thought of the two of us. In some alternative universe, she was my wife and I her husband. I didn't want to waste my life. The only way to do that was to live as honestly as I could and listen to the gut feeling in my stomach. The one that told me to speak the truth even when almost everybody would prefer that I remained silent.

When my dad returned from Pakistan, he hugged me, squeezing tighter than usual. 'I love you just the way you are and I will be here for you from now on,' he whispered. He held on to me as if he was scared to let me go, lest I disappear.

'It's terrible about Mariam, isn't it?' Uncle Tier said.

'I still can't really believe it. You hear about these things but you never think they actually happen to people you know,' I said.

'How's your dad doing?'

'He's still upset. I think it's really shaken him. He gives me such a hug every time we meet. Are you OK?'

'I'm fine,' he said, folding his arms over his now extraordinarily large belly.

'You look pregnant.'

'I feel pregnant.'

'Have the doctors said any more, Tier?' my mum asked. He had been off work with suspected tuberculosis.

'Not really. They aren't sure if it's TB.'

A few months later, on my birthday, my mum called and confirmed the news we'd all been dreading. Uncle Tier had cancer. Until then, cancer had been an advert on TV or a line in an obituary. Now it was happening to us. Uncle Tier had protected me when I was vulnerable and now he was in trouble and I didn't know how to help.

'The doctors have said it's Hodgkin's lymphoma,' Uncle Tier told me over the phone.

'What does that mean?'

'It's good news. Well, it's blood cancer, but apparently it's considered one of the most treatable forms of cancer. Survival rate is something like 95 per cent, so don't worry, OK? Just enjoy your birthday,' he said.

'Fuck my birthday.' He could hear from my voice I was trying to hold back the tears.

'Come on, Mohsin. I need you to be strong for your mum, and for my kids and for me. It's OK, it could have been a lot worse. Trust me, this is good news ... Also, they're draining my belly so no more pregnancy for me.'

'Only you could get cancer and tell me it's good news, Uncle Tier.'

That night, and for the first time in years, I prayed to God. Prayer wasn't a part of my life any more so it no longer came as naturally to me.

But Tier's diagnosis made it feel urgent. I decided to start talking to God again. I didn't use a prayer mat. I'd all but forgotten the religious rituals. But I sat on the floor, with my head to the ground. Although I hadn't used them in years, the Arabic prayers were still there, and finding them inside me, I also found some hope.

'Allah, I'm sorry I haven't spoken to you in years. And I'm sorry that I'm doing the thing I promised I wouldn't, which is to turn to you only when I need something. But please keep him safe. Please.'

36

I avoided Matthew, and when he called I was curt, if I answered at all. When we met up, it was apparent that the guy he knew was slipping through his fingers. Finally a message from him told me it was make or break. He wasn't prepared to chase me and wasn't sure where we had gone wrong. I knew I was pushing him away but I didn't know how to stop myself. It felt unmanageable to navigate a deeper intimacy with someone new when things with my family were so turbulent.

The problem was not that I didn't care about him, it was that I'd never felt like this about anyone before and I was terrified. I had become accustomed to keeping my two worlds apart but a partner, a boyfriend, would make that so much more difficult. It was as if I were juggling five balls already and he was trying to hand me three more.

'Look, if you don't want to do this then just say so.'

'No, it's not that. It's, it's ...' I didn't know what to say.

'Mohsin, you were the one who said you wanted us to be together properly and now suddenly you seem so distant.'

'I don't want this to end. I know I've been weird, I can't really explain it. Can you just give me a couple of days?' I said. I worried about my family, especially now that Uncle Tier was sick.

'Is this you doing the fade-out?' he said.

'The what?'

'You know, where you tell someone you need time and then slowly you disappear? Because I'd prefer it if you just ripped the plaster off, you know?'

'It's not that. I just need a few days, that's all,' I said, without conviction.

'OK,' he said.

'Dad, I need to talk to you.' We sat in the car outside the Tube station where he was about to drop me off.

'OK.'

'You know how you said I could talk to you about anything now?'

'I did.'

'Well … the truth is … I've met someone.'

'I know.'

'You know?' *What?*

'You think I don't know you. You're my son. It's difficult not to notice, Mohsin. You seem so … unburdened … not worrying so much about everything all the time,' he said. 'And you're nicer to your mum and me,' he added, laughing. I looked away.

'It's OK,' he said, leaning over to take my hand. 'What's his name?'

'Matthew … he's Irish,' I added quickly, as if his not being English might help my dad see him as less white. I had my own concerns about what it might mean for my cultural identity to be with someone from a different background but now was not the time to express them.

'They are very good people. Mohsin, you know what your mum is like but let me handle that. You live your life. Be happy.' Although I hadn't asked, I took that to mean he was fine with me finding a partner, but didn't want to meet Matthew. And I was too scared to push it.

*

A few months later, during which time Matthew and I had spent almost every day together, the tension I felt between my two worlds remained unresolved.

'Did you ask them about meeting me?' Matthew said.

'Not yet,' I replied.

'You said you were going to do it at the weekend.'

'And I was but you know my uncle's not very well and I don't want to rock the boat.' I couldn't tell him that my parents had sent word via Abbass that they weren't ready to meet him. Abbass said he would support me any way he could but that I should give up hope of my parents ever meeting Matthew. I hated keeping things from him. But there were things I had to protect him from because I didn't want him to hate them.

'That's not fair,' he said.

'What?'

'You're hiding behind your uncle's illness. You know that's not the reason you're stalling. We've been together nearly a year and they're still acting like I don't exist.'

'It's not personal,' I said.

'Oh, really? Are there any other people they're currently refusing to have anything to do with?'

'In my culture, just being gay is taboo. Can you imagine what having a boyfriend is like? It's taken me years, YEARS, to get them to a place where I can even tell them that you exist.'

'You're always so protective of them.'

'They're my family. Of course I'm going to protect them.'

'And what about me? What am I in all this?' His words were challenging. They forced me to think about things in a way I hadn't before.

'You have to trust me. I can't force it through.'

'So when then? When we move in together? Get married? Have kids? Are you going to hide me and our children away to protect your family then too?'

'Are you proposing to me?' I said.

'Oh please … you should be so lucky,' he said. 'You mean a lot to me, but you drive me mad.'

'Uncle Tier, you have to return this, I can't accept it.' It was a gold-rimmed watch with a white face, black roman numerals and a black strap.

'I hope you've finally learned your Roman numerals. And bollocks I'm returning it. You need it for when you're in court, I told you.'

'You shouldn't be spending money on things like this right now.'

'It's mainly from your nan! Mohsin, you're a barrister now. You've made us all very proud and this is our way of showing you. OK?'

'OK.'

'How's your fella?' I had taken a week off work to help him with a few things around the house and to spend time with him. I knew being stuck at home would be difficult for my uncle. He had such a sharp mind, such a vibrant enthusiasm for life, and I worried how cancer might affect his positivity, but he appeared to be resilient.

'Matthew's good,' I said.

'I can't wait to meet him. When I'm a bit better me and your auntie will put on a dinner.'

'I'd really like that, Uncle Tier.'

'Come on, Mohsin, you don't need to get upset,' he said, hugging me. 'OK, let's go. I've got an appointment with the grim reaper.' That was the nickname he gave his oncologist.

*

Just like everyone else, at Christmas we got together as a family to eat too much food, sing poorly pitched karaoke and argue about whether to watch the Queen's message. This year was still about all of those things but so much more. It was about supporting my uncle and helping to distract him from his daily struggle with cancer.

George Michael's death on Christmas Day 2016 was an unexpected blow. He was Uncle Tier's icon. I resisted the urge to talk about it, keen to avoid the suggestion that their fates were in any way entwined, but the headline was like a grenade, launched from the TV.

'What a waste,' he said, almost whispering to himself, from the sofa he was lying on, still in his pyjamas.

Now that I was self-employed, taking time off and working around his hospital appointments became much easier. Traditional chemotherapy seemed to all but eradicate the cancer, but he needed what the doctor somewhat ironically called the 'killer blow' and was referred to University College Hospital for specialist treatment. It was comforting to think of him receiving care from one of the world's best cancer centres and just a few stops down the Central Line.

'What about him?' Uncle Tier asked, his eyes darting in the direction of a handsome young doctor on the ward.

'We aren't here so I can pick up guys. Besides, I'm with Matthew.'

'Oh yes, of course ... but you can still window-shop. I'm just saying, he's a pretty sexy doctor, you know, and I'm pretty sure he bats for your team. I just want to know whether you think I've got good taste in blokes,' he said.

'Don't let Mum hear you say that.' I massaged his arms.

'Mohsin, your mum loves you more than anything and right now, son, she needs you. She doesn't cope well with all this, that's why I try and tell her to stay away.'

'I know … she doesn't listen,' I said.

'She's not perfect and I know she's not been there for you but you have to forgive her. This is too much for her right now.' He gestured towards the drip and tubes connected to his arm.

'You getting better is all that matters. My sexuality is just bullshit compared to this, I just wish she could see that.'

'I'll speak to her but listen to me. Love her. Love her unconditionally, the same way you would expect her to love you.'

37

I had few positive examples of romantic love. All of my grandparents met on their wedding days. My parents had met a handful of times before their arranged marriage. The relationships I had grown up around were based on cultural expectations and religious values. In that world, romantic love was the plaything of Bollywood drama, not of real life.

With Matthew, it was different. I could see all of his beauty and yet he remained a mystery to me. Until then I hadn't truly known the feeling of home but I found it there, in him. Culturally the sight was quite odd. Two men together. But we weren't two men. We were Matthew and Mohsin.

Instead of taking him to meet my family, I had taken Matthew to Oxford to meet Maureen. The two of us went punting on Cherwell River, in the summer sun. Matthew's smile radiated a golden sunlight that warmed every part of me.

'MZ,' he said lazily, as we watched the odd cloud pass by, 'don't you think the world would be a much better place if human beings had tails like dogs, which wagged uncontrollably when they were happy? That way they couldn't hide their feelings so easily.'

In that moment, I could barely contain my own emotion. I always prepared for the worst and feared that I might ruin things by saying something stupid.

'Matthew ... I love you,' I said. I knew I loved him because he was in my head and in my heart even when he wasn't around. In love songs, I heard him. In love scenes, I felt him. And in old couples, I saw the future of us. Much like the emotion, the words came effortlessly and I glimpsed a life lived without complexity.

'I love you too,' he said.

Matthew moved in soon after our trip to Oxford. It wasn't until this point that I got the full picture of what made him tick. His numerous, identical, white T-shirts, the skinny ties he must have bought when they were still in fashion, the magazines he'd worked on, the books that had made him laugh, made him cry. Now they were all in my home and so was he. He loved checking the post, something I despised. I learned he was an eternal optimist, hopeful that something magical, something other than another bill, might pop out of those plain white envelopes.

In the middle of the night I would sometimes reach over to make sure he was still there. Each morning when I woke up next to him, I was filled with excitement at the thought that it might always be this way. I loved him. But the life we were creating for ourselves continued to have a cloud hanging over it.

'Your family still don't know I live here?' Matthew said a couple of weeks after moving in.

'No,' I replied.

'They have keys, don't they?'

'Yes.'

'Don't you think you need to tell them? They are in for a bit of a shock if they catch me wandering around in my boxers.'

I told my parents to stop coming over unless they were prepared to meet him, but at the same time I didn't want them to feel like they were no longer welcome in my home. I would only invite them over when Matthew was away with work. One such evening my mum hovered awkwardly in the kitchen. I realised I'd forgotten to remove a picture of

Matthew stuck to the fridge door. It was taken at Pride. I had jumped on his back and was giving him a kiss on the cheek with my arms wrapped around him. I saw my mum's eyes glimpse the photo and then look away. Perhaps it was about time she saw how happy I was.

'Yeah, I definitely want to get married one day,' Matthew said to one of our friends. We were out to dinner. 'It's important to me, the commitment means something. And I guess I was brought up with it too.'

Although he was addressing the question of another, his answer was for my benefit. Marriage was a subject that we had not discussed. I knew it was important to him but, without my family, it meant nothing to me. What would it look like? Two men of different colours, different religions. Would I wear Western clothes at my own wedding or be the only one in traditional dress? The idea of marriage intruded on so many other areas that it was hard to consider.

'Absolutely not,' I said.

'What?' Matthew replied.

'No way!' I said.

'Why is this upsetting you?' he asked. We were having our first argument.

'It's not ... it's just ... you can't.'

'Why not?'

'Because ...'

'Because why, Mohsin?'

'Because it's bad enough that I have to introduce my family to a white guy one day. The idea that you would be a vegetarian would just make things even worse.'

He laughed. 'Are you kidding? You're not kidding. This is insane.'

'I'm not joking.'

'So you expect me to hold off becoming a vegetarian because your parents who, by the way, still refuse to meet me, might one day change their minds, and assuming that they do, it might upset them that I don't eat animals?' It was ridiculous but the idea of alienating myself or him any further was inconceivable. Telling them he was a vegetarian would make him even whiter than his already pale Irish skin.

But the argument wasn't about vegetarianism. He was beginning to resent the wall between him and the rest of me. I did too but I blamed it on culture, not on them, and when he couldn't understand, I blamed it on him, on the fact that he wasn't Pakistani.

'Imagine if his parents had refused to meet you because of your race, Mohsin. Surely you can understand why he feels upset by all of this?' Maureen said during a visit I made to Oxford by myself a week later. In an instant, I did understand. Our love wasn't just something that existed between the two of us. It existed independently of us. It aged, matured, it would endure its own peaks and troughs. Would he ever be able to celebrate Eid with us, go to my parents' house, eat my mum's food? These days I was spending so much time in hospital and I couldn't even ask him to come inside. And so he waited, dutifully, outside, where I would meet him and cry in his arms before returning to Uncle Tier's bedside. He understood that this was more important than anything else, why couldn't my mum?

The idea she held of Matthew was nothing like the man he was. It hurt that someone who inspired such love in me could conjure up such fear in her. When I was a child, my mum and dad would help me get to sleep by taking me for a drive around the block. I relaxed best when there was movement. I found movement comforting, reassuring in some way. Through all of this that's what was missing. I felt stuck.

'Hello, Mohsin, welcome to my pad.' Uncle Tier had lost even more weight. 'I always wanted to live in central London.' I looked out onto his view of the skyline. 'How are things at Pride?' he asked. 'I've resigned but that's not important.' The UCL doctors had confirmed the day before that the latest treatment had failed but they were going to try a stem cell transplant. I felt choked by the fear of losing him.

'You know, I'm not saying I'm there yet, I'm not, but I can see now why people stop fighting ... why they give up.'

I said nothing, not wanting to say the wrong thing. In my head I was willing him never to stop fighting.

'I want you to know something. In Islam it's important to get married and I want that for you and Matthew.'

'Uncle Tier, I don't think –'

'Listen to me please,' he said, taking my hand. 'I know you've struggled with your faith but I've had hours of lying in these beds and I've been close to God. You are not going to hell for the way you were born, OK? You have to know it. Another thing. I told your mum that my situation is getting worse and that I am asking this of her. I told her that I want her to meet Matthew. For me if not for you. Seeing me like this has changed her. I think she gets it now, what's important and what's not. She's agreed, Mohsin. She's agreed to meet Matthew.'

38

Cancer destroys everything. Love and hope and joy and all in between. It is a nuclear bomb exploding slowly, incrementally. Its unpredictability breeds terror. A terror that runs deep and hangs on. And yet, it is cancer that would ultimately lead me to this day. A request made by a brother to his big sister.

It was a short journey on this summer 2017 day, Matthew and I travelling only six stops on the Central Line to get to my parents' house, but it had taken what felt like my whole life to get there. I had spent so long preparing him and them for this moment I hadn't paused to wonder whether I was ready.

We stood on the doorstep of my family home. I was about to cross the threshold for the first time as an independent adult. The vibrant pinks and purples of the dusk sky seemed like a colourful welcome. Matthew gave my hand a squeeze before ringing the bell.

My dad opened the door and ushered us in.

'Where's Mum?' I asked. He frowned and my heart sank. She wasn't there. She had pulled out of today and away from me. And I would do the same. This would be the final straw. The camel dead.

'Hello.'

I heard before I saw her. Her strained smile belied her real emotions.

'Come in, come in,' she said, shaking Matthew's hand. I couldn't recall ever seeing her shake anyone's hand, and yet here she was, holding the man I loved at arm's length.

Matthew and I sat on one sofa, my parents on the other, under family portraits of weddings and graduations. The fact that my picture had not been removed from that wall served as a reminder that what was happening right now was valid and possible.

Watching Matthew with my parents was disconcerting, but my heart, long divided now felt whole. It was beating properly, neither part out of sync with the other. Every bit of me slowly coming together.

'So you have a *good* room too,' Matthew said. My parents looked puzzled. 'In Ireland we have a *good* room. It's only ever for guests and Mohsin tells me this is yours.'

'Yes, actually we rarely come in here,' my dad said, smiling.

I remembered coming out to my dad, years before, in this very room. This was the room in which I had hugged Mum, inconsolable with grief for the loss of her dutiful boy.

'Matthew, would you like some tea?' my dad asked. That question could help with the toughest of moments in England, Ireland or Pakistan.

'Oh yes please, I'd love a cup,' Matthew replied.

'What colour do you like your tea … ?' my dad began.

'No, Dad, please don't …'

'Just not this white please,' Matthew said, pointing to his face. My mum seemed to surprise herself with a giggle. I stopped holding my breath.

At the dinner table, I caught her staring at him until she caught me staring at her. *He's kind, he's thoughtful, he's a good man*, I wanted to whisper to her. I wanted her to see him the way I and everyone who knew him did, the way he deserved to be seen.

I watched as my mum served Matthew her spinach curry, the dish she made whenever I needed comforting. Her choice was a gesture, her way of telling me that she was really trying.

I piled yogurt onto the side of his plate and used my eyes to indicate he take some with each mouthful. At any other time, a white man turning red from eating spicy food would have been a source of amusement, but today I feared it would highlight his foreignness, another reminder of how different Matthew was to them in every conceivable way.

'I think you should serve Mohsin soon. He's hungry,' Matthew said.

'Oh, so you've encountered his hunger then?' my mum asked.

'Yeah! It's mad. Once he threatened to break up with me because he got home and I hadn't started dinner yet,' Matthew said.

'I believe you ... he's like Jekyll and Hyde when his stomach is empty,' my mum said.

'Well, more just Hyde and grumpier Hyde, I find,' Matthew said. My parents both laughed. He was no longer a concept, he was a person. A normal person. As they gradually began to see him for who he was, they began to show him who they were, to reveal the beauty of their true colours.

'Matthew,' my mum said, looking at him from across the dinner table after we had finished eating, 'I'm sorry it's taken us so long to meet ... it shouldn't have.'

'It's OK, honestly.'

'No, it isn't. I am sorry. You know about my brother being sick ...' She paused to hold back tears. My dad put his arm around her. 'I ... I want to thank you for supporting Mohsin. I told Tier I never wanted Mohsin to be lonely. I'm glad he's found you,' she said.

'Do you want another cup of tea before you go?' my mum asked at the end of the evening. Something told me she wasn't ready to say goodbye to the charming Irishman yet.

'You must come again soon. We want you to know you are always welcome here,' my dad said.

Matthew held out his hand to Mum, but instead she opened her arms and gave him a hug. As she did, I could sense warmth and authenticity in her embrace.

'He's very handsome,' she whispered into my ear, as I pulled on my jacket. I had no idea how to respond.

It was important to me that Uncle Tier meet the man who would shape my future. It was also important to me that Matthew meet Uncle Tier, the man who had helped shape so much of my present. It seemed incomprehensible that their window of time together might be so limited.

'How tall are you then?' my uncle asked from his hospital bed.

'About six three,' Matthew replied.

'Hmm, I'm not sure how I feel about that. I'm meant to be the tall one in the family.'

We all laughed nervously. My mum sat next to her brother, holding his hand.

'Matthew, I want you to take good care of him, OK?' he said. He spoke of a future in which he might not feature. There was a palpable sadness in the air for the relationship that might never be. These two wonderful men saying hello while silently acknowledging the possibility it was also goodbye.

'He can be stubborn as hell but he has a golden heart. Anyway, I've heard you know how to handle him, but if you ever need backup you come to me. This is not goodbye, I will see you again, I will.'

'That was the highlight of my day,' Uncle Tier said afterwards. He was emotional and I tried my hardest not to be. I told myself it was for his sake but it was for mine. If I started to cry I might never stop. That night, I prayed. Fourteen years ago, I asked God for a cure. Here I was again asking for the same thing. But more than anything I prayed for Uncle Tier to find peace.

When the news came that the latest medical trial hadn't worked, Uncle Tier went home. He didn't think he'd make it to his fiftieth birthday but he did. I took the day off work and went up to Northampton to spend his birthday with him. I returned to London on the Saturday evening. He died the following day. Those last few days taught me that dying was the loneliest thing I would ever have to do but that didn't mean I would have to do it alone.

Stars continue to shine even after they have died and the light from Uncle Tier's star felt the same. In the year following his death, I set up a support group for the families of LGBT Muslims. My parents needed help through their own coming out to the community, but there was almost no one who had gone before them, not openly. So we created something out of nothing.

On a Saturday afternoon, in a small venue in London, a dozen or so Muslim mothers, fathers, brothers and sisters sat in a circle, talking about their experiences with an LGBT relative. As the session got under way, nearly every person present spoke of how hard things were. How much pain their relative's sexuality had caused and the shame they feared it would bring.

'My brother was sick,' my mum said. The room fell silent. 'And it ... he has taught me a lot.' She still spoke of him in the present tense before catching herself. I took a deep breath and held it. 'We have so little time with our loved ones. Why waste it? God created my son this way and it is me who had the problem, not him.' I was stunned. My dad, noticing the tremble in my mum's voice, shuffled closer and put his arm around her.

'Children are not ours to disown,' he said. 'My son is not hurting anyone. He is a good person. I don't care what anybody says. I know that Allah loves him like I do.'

The dispiriting atmosphere in the room had jolted my parents into fighting for hope, for everyone, even if that hadn't been their intention.

'Mohsin is with Matthew,' my dad told the group. 'We have met him several times and he is a member of our family now. We didn't want to meet him but we did and we are glad we did. Our son is happy and he is with someone who we love too.' Matthew had proved the Trojan Horse that had allowed the gay me to enter their hearts at the same time that he did.

A few days after the support group meeting, I felt emboldened by their words to raise another difficult subject with my parents.

'Mum, Dad, I need to talk to you,' I said. We were about to head off to the shops.

'Oh my God, what now?!' my dad joked.

'I … I'm thinking of marrying Matthew.' I gulped. 'It's important to him and to me but I don't want to do it without knowing you two are OK with it,' I said. I avoided their gaze, worried about seeing disapproval in their expressions.

'OK with it?' My mum leaned in towards me and grabbed my hand. 'Mohsin, please hurry up before he dumps you!'

'And gets snapped up by someone else,' my dad added. My mum took my hand. 'The family have lost one great man but we are gaining another.'

My mum produced a childhood photo of me. 'I can't believe my little Mochie is getting married,' she said.

'Well, he hasn't said yes yet, Mum.'

I took the picture from my mum and stared at the boy in the white shirt. I'd been unable to look at photos from my childhood for a long time. When I did, I found myself wanting to leap inside the picture and protect the child from what was to come. But this time I felt a sense of excitement for him.

During our shopping trip, I told them I had to run an errand and would meet them in ten minutes.

'Where are you going? Are you going in there to look at wedding rings?' my mum asked.

'Maybe,' I replied, still unable to comprehend that these things could be spoken out loud, without the fear of inflicting pain.

'Well, I'm coming with you,' she said.

'Me too!' my dad said.

I looked at them from across the shop floor, as they perused the glass counters together. The thing about superheroes is that they had to have a weakness. If they were invincible, there would be no point. I knew now that the same was true in real life. What made them so special was that they found a way to overcome their kryptonite, not that they didn't have it in the first place.

Although Lapland's crisp winter air was invigorating, it did little to settle my nerves. On the turbulent flight over, Matthew's presence calmed my anxieties but these were nerves of a different kind. As we approached our treehouse, a giant cube with a facade made entirely of mirrors rendering it almost invisible to the eye, he gasped. I'd picked the 'mirrorcube' tree-house because it spoke to his love of design and also his love of the outdoors.

That night, wrapped in several layers of clothing, I led Matthew to a spot on a mound near the treehouse to try and catch a glimpse of the

Northern Lights. For Romans, the Northern Lights symbolised the dawn of a new day. For others, they were the dancing spirits of the dead.

Apart from the snow crunching satisfyingly beneath our boots, it was soundless. The green hue of the Northern Lights teased us with their presence but didn't quite come out from behind a landscape dominated by pine trees.

'Don't worry,' I said, 'we might see them tomorrow.'

'Where are we going?' Matthew asked the following evening. He protected his head from whipping branches as our snowmobile skidded past a huddle of trees. The stars decorated the dark sky like fairy lights, twinkling and shooting just for us. As we drove across Sweden's largest river, now completely frozen over, the orange blur in the distance soon became six orange blurs and then flames that lined the entrance to a white tepee.

'Look,' I said, pointing.

The green sky above our heads swirled and flickered with light. I imagined a George Michael song playing in the heavens. From the wireless speaker I had snuck into my jacket, I played Matthew's favourite song by the National. His eyes welled up.

The tepee had a wood-burning stove in the centre. To the side was a dining table with a candelabra and chairs. We trod carefully to our seats, over the frozen river beneath us.

'Matthew ...'

'Yes?'

'You know how you said you wished we could dream together?'

'Yes ...'

'Well, I think we already are.' The Japanese believe in repairing broken pottery with golden powdered resin. The shattered pieces are put back together and its defect becomes the thing that makes it more beautiful. I was born whole but quickly broken into separate pieces and had, ever since, worked hard to find a way of gluing the pot together, even when the pieces refused to fit. Matthew effortlessly put the fragments into place for me; he was my golden resin.

I took out the gold ring, handpicked by my parents, and the necklace with the ivory-coloured, heart-shaped stone I'd found on a Thai beach fifteen years earlier.

'Will you marry me?' I asked.

'Yes,' he said.

Epilogue

Once you've come out to your Pakistani Muslim parents, nothing is scary. At least that's what I assumed until I started contemplating my thoughts and experiences finding their way out of my mind and into the world. I can't give a straight answer as to why I wrote *A Dutiful Boy*.

In darker moments, I think it's about rage. About refusing to accept things for the way they are instead of the way they should be. About the grossly uneven playing field on which some of us try to play fairly. About the idea that any of this, any part of me should remain hidden away. But actually I think it's more about letting go of that rage rather than inflicting it.

I have carried this story for a long time. Writing these words brought a profound sense of relief, as if I have finally unburdened my shoulders and laid the heavy weight of it all onto these pages.

As a criminal barrister, my job is to tell a story. I tell my client's version, drawing together different threads to present a beginning, a middle and an end. My opponent does the same and then we leave it to the jury to decide which version they find more convincing. A story can send someone to prison. It can be the tale of a life ruined and the telling of it can also ruin lives. But I don't think a person has to be in front of a jury for their story to have meaning, for it to be told in the name of what is fair and just.

It hasn't been easy. At times I've felt somewhat like the canary, willingly lowering myself into the coal mine. There has been many a sleepless night wondering whether I am doing the right thing. No doubt there will be more. I have always been a worrier. I'm not sure if it's in my nature or in my circumstance. Either way, I worry. I am used to living in a state of anxious anticipation, holding my breath for the next calamity. I pause to consider what safety feels like, and wonder whether I feel it now. Whether now is the time to just breathe.

My worries used to be about *who* I was – the little Muslim boy, the young gay man, the lawyer fighting for what is right when so much feels wrong, the son wanting to be loved – but those parts of me have found peace. In some ways it was easier when there were barriers in front of me because the only thing I could do was climb over them. And I didn't climb alone. A series of sure footings and people's support helped me to make it over each hurdle. Without these links, this chain of people, things could have turned out very differently for me. And now the future feels promisingly uncertain.

But rather than be concerned with what might come next for me – married life, the hope of children, a deluge of tweets telling me how wrong I am – my worries have become societal; larger, uglier and more confronting. They are about things I want to achieve but cannot accomplish by myself. It's overwhelming to think of the millions of untold or half-told stories that have come before mine; of young men either throwing themselves or being thrown off buildings because of who they are; of black and brown queer people murdered in places that are supposed to protect them; and of children too scared to go to school because adults at the school gates are protesting against an inclusive education.

It's even more overwhelming to think of the millions of stories that will come after this one. Including from those same children stopped at the school gates, who will grow up hating themselves for something over which they have no choice, no control.

I fear that many of these stories will feature greater struggles, with less certain outcomes than mine, and how compounding this fear is with a resurgence of populism taking place in the background. Despite this, I am full of hope. I interview potential undergraduates applying for law at my old Oxford college. Asking questions of anxious young people sat in the same place I sat seventeen years ago. I wonder where their stories will take them.

We each have a story to tell. We've each felt like the outsider, with onlookers twitching from behind their curtains in judgement, as we stand alone in the street. So what are these stories? I have a feeling there is a lot to be learned by listening to them.

Nelson Mandela said that things can always seem impossible until they're done. I was unwilling to give up on my parents. And I am equally unwilling to give up on the idea that things can change. Of course, this book won't change the world but when we are young we need to see pictures of what's possible. An image that we can hold on to as we pull ourselves up into adulthood. One ambition of mine is that a few of the characters in this book can paint the picture that might spark conversations to change things for the better.

But this story is one set in the past. I am a governor of my old school, I am a trustee of Stonewall, I am a barrister and, now, I am the author of a memoir. Why? Because what matters is not this story, not my story, but the story of what happens next.

Resources for Support[*]

Note, using a special browser will prevent any searches from coming up in the Internet search history.

Albert Kennedy Trust helps with young people who are at risk or who have been made homeless because they are LGBT+: www.akt.org.uk/purple-door

Galva-108 is a non-profit religious organisation offering positive information and support to LGBTI Vaishnavas and Hindus: www.galva108.org/about-galva-108

Hidayah is a charitable organisation that runs projects and activities for LGBT+ Muslims: www.hidayahlgbt.co.uk

Imaan is a peer support group for LGBT+ Muslim charity (they also have the IMAAN forum where you can create an anonymous account and ask questions): imaanlondon.wordpress.com

The Inclusive Mosque Initiative is dedicated to creating places of worship for marginalised communities, spiritual practice and the promotion of inclusive Islamic principles. They run a support group for the families of LGBT+ Muslims: www.inclusivemosque.org

[*] This page was up to date as of November 2019. Most of these organisations are based in the United Kingdom. Inclusion on this list is not an endorsement of the organisation or all of its views.

KeshetUK's mission is to ensure that Jewish LGBT+ people and their families are included throughout Jewish life in the UK: www. keshetuk.org

LGBT Foundation is a charity delivering advice, support and information services to LGBT communities: Helpline: 0345 3 30 30 30 (open Monday to Friday between 10 a.m. and 6 p.m.) www.lgbt.foundation/helpline

LGBT Switchboard provides a one-stop listening service for LGBT+ people on the phone, by email and through Instant Messaging: Helpline: 0300 330 0630 (open 10 a.m. to 10 p.m. every day). www. switchboard.lgbt

Metropolitan Community Churches is an inclusive denomination with a network of affiliated churches worldwide. Their website contains a comprehensive (but not exhaustive) database of contact details for inclusive churches in every region of the world: www.mccchurch.org/overview/ourchurches/find-a-church

Naz offers counselling, support groups and sexual health advice, in particular for people from LGBT+ BAME communities: www.naz.org.uk

Sarbat is a volunteer led group addressing LGBT issues from a Sikh perspective: www.sarbat.net

Stonewall is a LGBT+ charity that campaigns for the equality of lesbian, gay, bi and trans people across Britain: www.stonewall.org.uk

UK Black Pride is Europe's largest celebration for LGBTQ people of African, Asian, Caribbean, Middle Eastern and Latin American descent. They also host activities throughout the year: www.ukblackpride.org.uk

Thank You

Maureen, I'm here because of you. I hope I can one day do for someone what you have done for me.

To Sienna and the Penguin WriteNow team, for the brilliant scheme that made this book possible. To my fellow WriteNow mentees, for the group therapy. To my agent, Cathryn Summerhayes, who offered to mentor me before having read a word of my writing. To Ajda Vucicevic for getting me to tell my story and to Rowan Yapp, Noor Sufi, Alex Russell, Mireille Harper, Ryan Bowes, Alison Davies and everyone at VINTAGE, for helping me do it. Arzu Tahsin for the invaluable edits and advice. To Afua and the other MZ, for reading the book and all the brilliant ideas. Louise Mountain at Cuba Pictures, for believing in the book from the beginning.

To my Stonewall colleagues for the encouragement, you are an inspiring group of people. Richard Summerscales, Ros Earis and everyone at 6KBW College Hill, thank you for the supportive environment.

To all my teachers but in particular Ms Marsh-Feiley, Mr Houghton and Ms Lupton. And Ed Peel, for seeing something I couldn't.

To my friends, I wish I could name you all because along the way you have become my family too. Ish, Clare, Alicia, Sinead, Felicity, Yasmin, Elsa, Alex, Dalia Mohsen, Charlie, Heather, Kevin, Jeff, Brian, Andrew, Louis, Nicholas, Renaud, Adam, Mitch, Christina and James. Marya, we have grown up together and it was a lot less frightening with you there.

To my family, I am lucky to be a part of our unit. Abbass, you will always be my first phone call. To my sister-in-law, for showing Aya the power of books. Raza, I'm proud of the man you are becoming.

Ami, you have never stopped. Not for a minute. And it's all for us. Dad, you instilled strong values in each of us. You've shown that family is more important than anything else. The example you have both set will mean more than you might ever know.

Mamu Tier, I will always need you. I wish you were still here.

MPAJ, for everything but especially the dancing. I can't wait to get married. To my new family, thank you for already making me feel so welcome.

And finally, you the reader. Thank you for your time. The first audience for everything in this book were the people I love, many of whom are mentioned on this page. I hope that *A Dutiful Boy* helps you tell your story to the people you love.

Mohsin